Lecture Notes in Computer Science   14208

Founding Editors

Gerhard Goos
Juris Hartmanis

Editorial Board Members

Elisa Bertino, *Purdue University, West Lafayette, IN, USA*
Wen Gao, *Peking University, Beijing, China*
Bernhard Steffen, *TU Dortmund University, Dortmund, Germany*
Moti Yung, *Columbia University, New York, NY, USA*

The series Lecture Notes in Computer Science (LNCS), including its subseries Lecture Notes in Artificial Intelligence (LNAI) and Lecture Notes in Bioinformatics (LNBI), has established itself as a medium for the publication of new developments in computer science and information technology research, teaching, and education.

LNCS enjoys close cooperation with the computer science R & D community, the series counts many renowned academics among its volume editors and paper authors, and collaborates with prestigious societies. Its mission is to serve this international community by providing an invaluable service, mainly focused on the publication of conference and workshop proceedings and postproceedings. LNCS commenced publication in 1973.

Kejiang Ye · Liang-Jie Zhang
Editors

Internet of Things – ICIOT 2023

8th International Conference
Held as Part of the Services Conference Federation, SCF 2023
Shenzhen, China, December 17–18, 2023
Proceedings

Springer

Editors
Kejiang Ye
Chinese Academic of Sciences
Beijing, China

Liang-Jie Zhang ⓘ
Shenzhen Entrepreneurship and Innovation
Federation
Shenzhen, China

ISSN 0302-9743   ISSN 1611-3349 (electronic)
Lecture Notes in Computer Science
ISBN 978-3-031-51733-4   ISBN 978-3-031-51734-1 (eBook)
https://doi.org/10.1007/978-3-031-51734-1

This Springer imprint is published by the registered company Springer Nature Switzerland AG
The registered company address is: Gewerbestrasse 11, 6330 Cham, Switzerland

Paper in this product is recyclable.

Preface

With the rapid advancements of mobile Internet, cloud computing and big data, device-centric traditional Internet of Things (IoT) is now moving into a new era which is termed Internet of Things Services (IOTS). In this era, sensors and other types of sensing devices, wired and wireless networks, platforms and tools, data processing/visualization/analysis and integration engines, and other components of traditional IoT are interconnected through innovative services to realize the value of connected things, people, and virtual Internet spaces. The way of building new IoT applications is changing. We indeed need creative thinking, long-term visions, and innovative methodologies to respond to such a change. The ICIOT 2023 conference was organized to promote research and application innovations around the world.

ICIOT 2023 was a member of Services Conference Federation (SCF). SCF 2023 had the following 10 collocated service-oriented sister conferences: 2023 International Conference on Web Services (ICWS 2023), 2023 International Conference on Cloud Computing (CLOUD 2023), 2023 International Conference on Services Computing (SCC 2023), 2023 International Conference on Big Data (BigData 2023), 2023 International Conference on AI & Mobile Services (AIMS 2023), 2023 World Congress on Services (SERVICES 2023), 2023 International Conference on Internet of Things (ICIOT 2023), 2023 International Conference on Cognitive Computing (ICCC 2023), 2023 International Conference on Edge Computing (EDGE 2023), and 2023 International Conference on Blockchain (ICBC 2023). As the founding member of SCF, the first International Conference on Web Services (ICWS) was held in June 2003 in Las Vegas, USA. Meanwhile, the First International Conference on Web Services - Europe 2003 (ICWS-Europe'03) was held in Germany in Oct, 2003. ICWS-Europe'03 was an extended event of the 2003 International Conference on Web Services (ICWS 2003) in Europe. In 2004, ICWS-Europe became the European Conference on Web Services (ECOWS), which was held in Erfurt, Germany.

This volume presents the accepted papers for the 2023 International Conference on Internet of Things (ICIOT 2023), held in Shenzhen during December 17–18, 2023. ICIOT 2023 received 28 submissions, and we accepted 8 papers for the proceedings. Each was reviewed and selected by at least three independent members of the ICIOT 2023 International Program Committee in a single-blind review process.

We are pleased to thank the authors whose submissions and participation made this conference possible. We also want to express our thanks to the Organizing Committee and Program Committee members, for their dedication in helping to organize the conference and reviewing the submissions. We look forward to your great contributions as a volunteer, author, and conference participant as part of the fast-growing worldwide services innovations community.

December 2023   Kejiang Ye
                                                                         Liang-Jie Zhang

Organization

General Chair

Haiying Shen   University of Virginia, USA

Program Chair

Kejiang Ye   Chinese Academy of Sciences, China

Services Conference Federation (SCF 2023)

General Chairs

Ali Arsanjani   Google, USA
Wu Chou   Essenlix Corporation, USA

Coordinating Program Chair

Liang-Jie Zhang   Shenzhen Entrepreneurship and Innovation
                            Federation, China

CFO and International Affairs Chair

Min Luo   Georgia Tech, USA

Operation Committee

Jing Zeng   China Gridcom Co., Ltd., China
Yishuang Ning   Tsinghua University, China
Sheng He   Tsinghua University, China

Steering Committee

Calton Pu (Co-chair)	Georgia Tech, USA
Liang-Jie Zhang (Co-chair)	Shenzhen Entrepreneurship and Innovation Federation, China

ICIOT 2023 Program Committee

Georgios Bouloukakis	Télécom SudParis, France
Na Yu	Samsung Research America, USA
Abhishek Bajpai	Rajkiya Engineering College, India
Satya Nagabhushana Rao Kamisetti	JNTUK, India
Marisol García-Valls	Universitat Politècnica de València, Italy
Abdurazzag Aburas	University of KwaZulu-Natal, South Africa
Françoise Sailhan	IMT-Atlantique, France
Haiying Shen	University of Virginia, USA
Kejiang Ye	Chinese Academy of Sciences, China
Hongsheng Chen	Hubei University of Science and Technology, China

Conference Sponsor – Services Society

The Services Society (S2) is a non-profit professional organization that has been created to promote worldwide research and technical collaboration in services innovations among academia and industrial professionals. Its members are volunteers from industry and academia with common interests. S2 is registered in the USA as a "501(c) organization", which means that it is an American tax-exempt nonprofit organization. S2 collaborates with other professional organizations to sponsor or co-sponsor conferences and to promote an effective services curriculum in colleges and universities. S2 initiates and promotes a "Services University" program worldwide to bridge the gap between industrial needs and university instruction.

The Services Sector accounted for 79.5% of the GDP of the USA in 2016. The Services Society has formed 5 Special Interest Groups (SIGs) to support technology- and domain-specific professional activities.

- Special Interest Group on Services Computing (SIG-SC)
- Special Interest Group on Big Data (SIG-BD)
- Special Interest Group on Cloud Computing (SIG-CLOUD)
- Special Interest Group on Artificial Intelligence (SIG-AI)
- Special Interest Group on Metaverse (SIG-Metaverse)

About the Services Conference Federation (SCF)

As the founding member of the Services Conference Federation (SCF), the first **International Conference on Web Services (ICWS)** was held in June 2003 in Las Vegas, USA. Meanwhile, the First International Conference on Web Services - Europe 2003 (ICWS-Europe 2003) was held in Germany in October 2003. ICWS-Europe 2003 was an extended event of the 2003 International Conference on Web Services (ICWS 2003) in Europe. In 2004, ICWS-Europe became the European Conference on Web Services (ECOWS), which was held in Erfurt, Germany. Sponsored by the Services Society and Springer, SCF 2018 and SCF 2019 were held successfully in Seattle and San Diego, USA. SCF 2020 and SCF 2021 were held successfully online and in Shenzhen, China. SCF 2022 was held successfully in Hawaii, USA. To celebrate its 21st birthday, SCF 2023 was held on September 23–26, 2023, in Honolulu, Hawaii, USA with Satellite Sessions in Shenzhen, Guangdong, China.

In the past 20 years, the ICWS community has been expanded from Web engineering innovations to scientific research for the whole services industry. The service delivery platforms have been expanded to mobile platforms, Internet of Things, cloud computing, and edge computing. The services ecosystem has gradually been enabled, value added, and intelligence embedded through enabling technologies such as big data, artificial intelligence, and cognitive computing. In the coming years, all transactions with multiple parties involved will be transformed to blockchain.

Based on technology trends and best practices in the field, the Services Conference Federation (SCF) will continue serving as the umbrella code name for all services-related conferences. SCF 2023 defined the future of New ABCDE (AI, Blockchain, Cloud, Big-Data, & IOT) and brought us into the 5G for Services Era. The theme of SCF 2023 was **Metaverse Era**. We are very proud to announce that SCF 2023's 10 co-located theme topic conferences all centered around "services", while each focused on exploring different themes (web-based services, cloud-based services, Big Data-based services, services innovation lifecycle, AI-driven ubiquitous services, blockchain-driven trust service-ecosystems, industry-specific services and applications, and emerging service-oriented technologies).

– Bigger Platform: The 10 collocated conferences (SCF 2023) were sponsored by the Services Society, which is the world-leading not-for-profit organization (501 c(3)) dedicated to the service of more than 30,000 worldwide Services Computing researchers and practitioners. A bigger platform means bigger opportunities for all volunteers, authors, and participants. Meanwhile, Springer provided sponsorship for best paper awards and other professional activities. All the 10 conference proceedings of SCF 2023 will be published by Springer and indexed in ISI Conference Proceedings Citation Index (included in Web of Science), Engineering Index EI (Compendex and Inspec databases), DBLP, Google Scholar, IO-Port, MathSciNet, Scopus, and zbMATH.

- Brighter Future: While celebrating the 2023 version of ICWS, SCF 2023 highlighted the Second International Conference on Metaverse (METAVERSE 2023), which covered immersive services for all vertical industries and area solutions. Its focus was on industry-specific services for digital transformation. This will lead our community members to create their own brighter future.
- Better Model: SCF 2023 will continue to leverage the invented Conference Blockchain Model (CBM) to innovate the organizing practices for all the 10 theme conferences. Senior researchers in the field are welcome to submit proposals to serve as CBM Ambassador for an individual conference to start better interactions during your leadership role in organizing future SCF conferences.

Contents

Contents

A Survey on Security in Data Transmission in IoT: Layered Architecture

Mandicou Ba[1,2,3]([✉]), Lang Dionlar[1,3], Bachar Salim Haggar[1,4], and Idy DIOP[1,2,3]

[1] Laboratoire d'Imagerie Médicale et de Bio-Informatique (LIMBI), Dakar, Senegal
[2] Unité de Modélisation Mathématiques et Informatique des Systèmes Complexes, N'Djamena, Tchad
[3] Ecole Superieure Polytechnique (ESP), Université Cheick Anta Diop (UCAD), Dakar, Senegal
{mandicou.ba,dionlar.lang,idy.diop}@esp.sn
[4] Ecole Nationale Supérieure des Technologies de l'Information et de la Communication (ENASTIC), N'Djamen, Tchad
b.haggar@enastic.td

Abstract. The Internet of Things (IoT) is the communications technology where, physical objects, which are basically not designed for connection, will be able to connect, create, receive and exchange collected data permanently and transparently. Many IoT applications focus on the automation of various tasks and try to encourage the interaction of inanimate physical objects to function without any human action. The various IoT applications hold great promise for enhancing the level of comfort, efficiency and authorisation for end users. This is the dream world towards which humans are working relentlessly. But succeeding in building such a world in its practical and growing implementation requires security, confidentiality and authentication always present and high. In this respect, rigorous work is needed on the structure of the various layers that make up the overall IoT architecture, in order to avoid existing risks and problems. In this survey, an in-depth look at the security of data transmission by layer and their solutions is presented. After discussing the security issues, advantages and disadvantages of the proposed solutions are also discussed. Finally, the limitations of IoT devices are presented.

Keywords: IoT · Security · Authentication · Authorization · Integrity · Availability · Cloud

1 Introduction

The Internet of Things (IoT) is a new concept, which not only facilitates the permanent connection of a large number of devices to the internet, but also provides a mechanism for controlling and managing these devices remotely [1]. The IoT is everywhere and an integral part of our everyday lives. The Internet of Things (IoT) represents a technological revolution that is transforming the way

K. Ye and L.-J. Zhang (Eds.): ICIOT 2023, LNCS 14208, pp. 1–17, 2024.
https://doi.org/10.1007/978-3-031-51734-1_1

we interact with the world around us. The Internet of Things (IoT) paradigm aims to make the Internet even more immersive and ubiquitous in our everyday lives. The Internet of Things (IoT) facilitates the development of a number of applications that will exploit the huge quantity and diversity of data generated by these objects to offer new services to citizens, businesses and administrations. This concept has applications in many areas of life, including home automation, industrial automation, medical aids, mobile healthcare, assistance for the elderly, intelligent energy management and smart grids, automobiles, traffic management, etc. [2]. The Internet of Things (IoT) is a new communications concept that envisions a future in which objects, machines and terminals are used permanently and optimally, while the heterogeneous nature of the various fields of application makes the task of choosing the right solution to meet the requirements of each application a magnificent challenge. All this difficulty has led to a multitude of different and sometimes incompatible solutions for the practical implementation of the Internet of Things (IoT). As a result, systematically, the practical implementation of the IoT network, the different services, and the network devices, have no established best practices for reasons of its novelty and complexity [3]. The full and everywhere practical implementation of the Internet of Things in various fields, can play a remarkable role and improve the quality of our daily lives. The Internet of Things enables physical objects to see, hear, think and perform tasks by making them « talk » together, share information and coordinate decisions. The Internet of Things transforms objects from the traditional to the intelligent by leveraging its foundation of technologies such as ubiquitous computing, embedded devices, communication technologies, sensor networks, internet protocols and applications [4]. That's why the security of this collected data is becoming a major concern in the world of technology these days. IoT implementations and devices are exposed to attacks that could compromise the confidentiality, integrity and availability of the data, as well as the security of the users (personal information) [5–7]. It is a question of examine the security issues in the different layers (perception or physical, network, middleware and application) of the protocol stack, identify the advantages and disadvantages of existing layered solutions and conclude the paper by reviewing the limitations of IoT devices.

2   Attacks and Their Solutions in the Layered IoT Architecture

According to many of the surveys, there are many architectures proposed for IoT by different researchers and most of them focus on middleware layer and network layer which deal with the necessities of IoT [5–7]. The basic architecture proposed for the IoT is shown in Fig. 1, namely the perception layer, the network layer, the middleware layer and the application layer. All of these layers must communicate for the proper transmission of data, from its remote collection to its action on the environment, via the network and the Internet. There are different layered attacks and their existing solutions that we will try to present in this section.

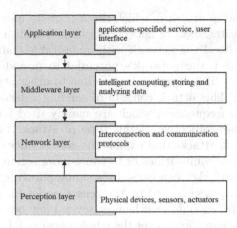

Fig. 1. General IoT architecture

3 Attacks and Solutions at the Perception Layer

The perception or physical layer comprises all the devices connected in an IoT network, such as sensors, RFIDs, the wireless sensor network (WSN), GPS, etc., which are responsible for collecting information and identifying them [9,11,12]. Attacks in this layer are recurrent, and there are also some attempts at solutions to block the way to curious and malicious intentions [13].

3.1 Attacks on the Perception or Physical Layer

The different targets of attack and the most common problems in this layer are variable and multiple [13]. The sensitive problem with the perception layer is node capture. An attacker can easily control a node such as a network gateway. He could extract critical information from it, for example cryptographic secrets on which the confidentiality and integrity of the network are based [5]. The other security issue for the perception layer is the detection of the anomalous sensor node. This can occur when the node is physically attacked (e.g. destroyed, disabled) or intruded/compromised by cyber attacks. These nodes are generally referred to as faulty nodes [?]. The worst attack that could damage the entire network would be an attack on the integrated sensors (functional sensors in a network). The most elementary active attacks in wireless sensor networks are the theft or destruction of sensors. Sensors are deployed in areas that cannot always be monitored. So a single individual can steal one or more sensors, or even destroy them. If a sensor is destroyed, the network must be able to adapt t o the new situation and avoid being divided into several sub-networks unable to communicate with each other. In addition, a stolen node may divulge certain information t o an attacker. It can just as easily be reprogrammed and reinserted into the network and thus become a malicious node, operating as a spy node as explained in [7–9]. Another attack in this layer is the Denis of Service (DoS) attack, which is a kind of attack in which the legitimate user is prevented from accessing emails, websites, data or network services. This is a situation in which attackers attempt to flood the network with undesirable traffic, malicious code and actions that weaken the network's potential to provide the programmed service: Malicious data. This layer is also exposed to other attacks such as communication jamming. This attack consists of sending a large number of noise signals over the radio frequencies, which are mainly used for RFID communication, and is the main objective of this type of attack [14]. The perception layer is very sensitive to attacks that exploit the accessibility of the transmission medium to intercept communications or to cause more serious problems such as the jamming that an attacker can cause by sending parasitic signals that interfere with the radio frequencies used by the sensor nodes for communication. If the attacker is powerful enough, or if he uses several low-power nodes, the communication disruption can spread over the whole network [5]. Also, in this layer, tampering with data may be in order and this may cause serious damage to the data transmitted over the network. Data tampering can be easily executed by an attacker in the event that unencrypted data is sent over the network. The lack of traffic encryption on the local network is often linked to the fact that this traffic is not visible from the outside. However, in a poorly configured local network, this may not be the case, which can lead to data leakage or loss [16]. Another perception layer security issue concerns the cryptographic algorithms and the key management mechanism to be used. The public key algorithm has been considered practical for authenticating nodes. It is more scalable and can better secure the entire network without a shared key management protocol [17]. Attacks on this layer also include attacks by key management mechanisms. As we explained earlier, it is not possible in wireless sensor networks to use complex cryptographic methods. The low power of the sensors does not allow it, and when it does, the calculation time is too long. However, it is possible to use simple cryptographic techniques with symmetric keys, as shown in [18]. According to this literature, there are four types of key cryptography used in this way: the global key, the key shared by a pair of nodes, the key shared by a group of nodes and the individual key.

3.2 Solutions Approaches in the Perception Layer

The proposed solutions are presented as follows: The authors of [19] proposed and evaluated a localised fault detection algorithm to identify faulty nodes in WSN. An improvement to the PKI-type security mechanism protocol for threats involving the security of nodes in IoT systems [20]. The authors of [21] proposed a model for a decentralized intrusion detection system for the WSN. In [22], the authors deduced the probability of intrusion detection in homogeneous and heterogeneous WSNs. An improved protocol for radio frequency identification (RFID) was developed [23]. Another security issue for the perception layer, according to [17], concerns the cryptographic algorithms and the key management mechanism to be used.The public key algorithm has been considered practical for authenticating nodes. It is more scalable and can better secure the entire network without a complicated key management protocol. Also in [24], three low-power public key encryption algorithms are the most promising candidates for wireless sensor networks.Key management includes the generation, distribution, storage, update and destruction of secret keys. The existing key distribution scheme can be divided into four groups: key broadcast distribution as in [18,25], Group Key Distribution according to [26,27], the pre-distribution of the master key and the distribution of keys in pairs as indicated in [28,29]. For the problem of resource-constrained Wireless Sensor Networks (WSN) in distributed IoT applications, the authors of [31] discussed the introduction of ubiquitous authentication protocols. Complicated Key Set and Scheme (PAuthKey), which allows different nodes to access the network from these keys.

4   Network Layer Attacks and Their Solutions

As the network layer transports a very large amount of data, it is very exposed to attacks that can cause "congestion network". What are the latest attacks? What are the various proposed solutions?

4.1   The Various Attacks on the Network Layer

The main security problems at this layer relate to the authentication and integrity of data transmitted over the network. Since it transports a large quantity of data, it is highly susceptible to security attacks such as :

- Replay attacks: an intruder copies a fragment or key of the messages, the two parties exchange information and steal it;
- DoS attacks: a type of attack in which the legitimate user is prevented from accessing email, websites, data or network services;
- Man-in-the-middle attacks: an intruder intervenes in a communication between two parties, either to eavesdrop or to impersonate both parties, and gains access to the information of the communicating parties;
- Malicious code injection: an attacker captures a functional node and injects it with malicious code, network access and control codes;
- Distributed Denial of Service (DDoS) attacks: a DoS attack in which one node is targeted by several compromised nodes, flooding the network with useless messages and malicious code, causing the service to be unavailable to the targeted users.

4.2   Existing Solutions for the Network Layer

The network layer is responsible for transmitting and processing data transmitted by sensors. According to various literatures, the solutions proposed to deal with the various problems or attacks in this layer can be based on: For the problem of authentication, identification and encryption of messages, the following solutions are proposed and discussed in the literature [32] of a mechanism that supports secure end-to-end communication between the Internet and IP sensor networks (including AH and ESP). To solve the problem of DDoS attacks, a lightweight algorithm was proposed in [33] to prevent DDoS attacks on the IoT network environment. For identity authentication problems, as indicated in [34], an identity-based authentication scheme is proposed to deal with the inherent heterogeneity in the IoT and to integrate the various protocols in the IoT (SDN). The solution to the problem of authentication for communicating with a resource-limited device was discussed in [35], consisting of the introduction of a mutual authentication architecture that allows resource-limited devices to use Datagram Transport Layer Security (DTLS). Also in the same literature, the authors proposed an appliance called the Internet of Things Security Support Provider (IoTSSP), which manages device certifications, provides authentication services and is also responsible for the authentication of devices, of the session establishment between the devices. In order to resolve the same attacks in this layer, a proposed solution as in [36], studied the hypothesis of using certificates and lightweights as security solutions for peer authentication in the IoT. The authors also analyzed the preliminary overhead reduction and discussed their applicability for the certificate-based DTLS handshake. Also analyze preliminary overhead reduction and discuss their applicability for certificate-based DTLS handshake. Three main ideas have been devised by the authors to reduce the general overheads of DTLS handshaking, which is based on session resumption, pre-validation and handshake delegation.

4.3   Attacks or Problems at the Middleware Layer and Their Solutions

The middleware or inter-software layer is the layer just above the network layer that carries out mass data processing and enables intelligent decisions to be made in the network. This layer uses advanced technologies such as cloud computing, large data processing and databases. The problem with this layer is the difficulty of managing all this mass data.

Attacks in the Middleware Layer. As in the other layers, the middleware layer also encounters difficulties in data flow management, and most of the literature describes problems such as: the difficulty of managing huge amounts of data: this layer has the particularity of processing huge amounts of data. Then, the more the quantity of this data increases, the more the layer finds it difficult to manage it normally, which causes harm to the network. There is also the added problem of the difficulty of recognising valid data and filtering out malicious information. The layer also has the ability and possibility to differentiate data belonging to the network (normal or valid data) from malicious data. However, the real problem with this function is the difficulty in recognising valid data and filtering malicious information introduced by the attacker. There is also another problem in this layer, namely the management of suspect data: The attacker replaces the data with malicious information to obtain a list of valid data and network information. This can lead to the transmission of invalid or malicious data instead of valid information, which can cause the network to fail or shut down completely.

Existing Middleware Solutions. The middleware layer is responsible for retrieving and processing the data and, above all, for making intelligent decisions, that's to say, based on the results obtained. One possible solution is to authenticate all the devices on the resource-limited network. Also, Given the huge amount of data to be processed, the cloud will have to be used for secure storage. In most of the literature, attempts to solve these problems in this layer revolve around: In [37], the security issue of access control and authentication has been addressed. Also in this literature, the authors proposed a scheme that takes into account the reduction in communication time between all cloud service providers and the traditional trusted third-party service. Always looking for a solution, in [38], it is discussed and introduces an encrypted query processing approach for storing IoT data securely on the cloud database, and also enabling query processing on the encrypted information. Finally, as a solution to solve the transmission problem between the cloud and smart devices, the use of an identity and service manager on the devices is proposed [39].

5 Attacks and Solutions in the Application Layer

The application layer comprises intelligent devices that enable end-users to have personalised services. These devices a r e generally simple, low-power and lightweight, making them highly vulnerable to attacks, programming errors or even repeated and varied mishandling. What are the possible solutions for resolving or minimising the damage caused by these attacks? The various literature's consulted not only list the attacks but also propose solutions, either to resolve them definitively or to minimise the damage caused by these attacks or problems, as described below.

5.1 Application Layer Attacks

In this sub-section, we look at the various attacks and some of the most recurrent problems of this layer in the various literature reviewed. One example is the malfunctioning of an application caused by bugs used by malicious attacks to replace the correct program code. This would subsequently lead to these applications being compromised or stopped, which would prevent them from providing what is programmed and also from executing authenticated services in an inappropriate manner. There is also the problem of access control, confidentiality and data leakage in the application layer, as this layer is responsible for sharing data. There is also the problem of software vulnerability, which is the consequence of weaknesses in the design, implementation or use of the system's software components, but in our specific case we are talking about malicious attacks, which use software to destroy or gain access to network or user data. Software vulnerability enables the attacker to fool the application, for example by bypassing access control checks or executing commands on the host system. Another attack is called a spear-phishing attack. This is a type of phishing attack, which involves targeting specific individuals or groups of individuals in the network. Spear phishers impersonate people they know and trust and try to trick them in to divulging information about themselves. These attacks can be used to steal sensitive information (such as account identifiers, e-mail, commercial secrets, card numbers, etc.), to download malicious software or, in short, to authorise certain tasks to be carried out. According to IBM's Cost of a Data Brench 2022 report in [40], spear phishing attacks were the second most common cause of data breaches in 2022. Malicious code attacks are dangerous codes or scripts that create vulnerabilities in the IoT application layer, which can lead to backdoors, security breaches and data theft. Malicious code is a self-executing application that can self-activate and present itself in various forms. This code then gives cybercriminals unauthorised remote access to the system under attack. Smart meter/network hacking attacks are unauthorised access in IoTs to a smart meter or its data transmissions in order to obtain information about the user, or to modify communications between devices. The list of attacks and problems at this layer is not exhaustive, there is also the inability to receive security patches which must be taken into account. This is the failure to apply software, driver or firmware updates in order to protect applications against certain vulnerabilities. The older the software, the more its vulnerabilities are exposed. This is the purpose of security patches and their distribution to operating systems and applications. All these attacks and problems can affect the proper operation of applications, leading to the modification, hacking or destruction of the data collected.

5.2   Solutions Again Application Layer Attacks

The application layer provides services to end users. It is in this layer that the exchange of multiple messages between the application and the end-users takes place. These different exchanges are possible thanks to several protocols in the context of IoT. As with message exchange in the traditional internet, the main and most widely used application layer message exchange protocols are well known. Message Queuing Teleme- try Transport (MQTT) is a publish-subscribe messaging protocol, a message publication and node subscription mechanism in which broadcasters do not a priori send messages to recipients. Instead, a category is associated with emitted messages without knowing whether there are any recipients. In the same way, recipients subscribe to the category that interests them and only receive the corresponding messages, without knowing whether there are any broadcasters. There are many MQTT agents available. They vary in their functionality and some of them implement additional features. Also the Contrained Application Protocol (CoAP) is present and used in this layer. It is a protocol that specifies the way in which low-power constrained peripherals operate in the Internet of Things (IoT). Developed by the IETF, CoAP is defined in IETF specification RFC 7252. CoAP is designed to enable simple, constrained pereipherals to use the IoT, even through constrained networks with low bandwidth and availability. There is also the Extensible Messaging Presence Protocol (XMPP). This is a set of standard protocols based on the TCP/IP protocol, using a client-server architecture that allows the use of multiple protocols. This is a way of exchanging instantaneous or non-instantaneous messages between clients in XML format. In the various literatures consulted, as in [41], the following is discussed. The authors of [42] proposed an architecture based on IoT-OAS focusing on http/CoAP services, which can be integrated using an external authorization service based on the oauth(pAS) protocol. [42] proposed, as a solution, a technique using inter-device authentication and session key distribution to secure inter-device communication. The same authors also proposed the use of this upstream key to prevent the replay attack and the man-in-the-middle attack. In [44], for the resolution of confidentiality and security problems in communication between devices, the authors proposed the security policy. In the literature [45], a privacy protection mechanism is proposed for IoT devices, because the primary mission of this layer is data. So the solutions proposed in this layer alone cannot solve the overall security problems in IoTs, but the devices manufactured must also take security and patches into account beforehand.

6   The Advantages and Disadvantages of Existing Solutions

As with all innovative technologies, the search for solutions to the problems encountered is crucial. The solutions proposed in the various literatures to prevent or minimise the attacks occurring in the various layers have both advantages and disadvantages. In one subsection, we list the different advantages of the different solutions per layer and in another, the disadvantages. This will enable us to see the various limitations of these solutions in the proposed literature.

6.1   The Advantages of the Proposed Solutions in the Layers

In this subsection, we focus on the advantages of the solutions proposed in the various layers in a global way, simply by indicating, each time the layer concerned:

The Perception Layer. The perception layer is the layer in which we find various divices for retrieving data or acting on the environment, such as: sensors, RFIDs, GPS, wireless sensor networks (WSNs), etc. According to [19], the solution to the challenge of identifying compromised sensors in wireless networks, using the algorithm, provides maximum precision and the false rate is minimal in detecting faulty sensors in WSNs. Another advantage of this solution is that the complexity of this algorithm is low, which leads to fluidity in understanding the process. The solution proposed in [20] for node security, which is to use the PKI-type security protocol mechanism, is also advantageous because it improves the security mechanism. To secure RFIDs, the authors of [23], n their solution, which is a protocol for identification by radio frequency, is computationally better and prevents disclosure and desynchronization attacks. In [45], light security (RFID) encryption gives more efficiency and considerably reduces the communication cost. For constrained resources, the solution proposed in [31], which uses the PAuthKey protocol for authentication and key establishment, allows different end users to authenticate themselves directly to the sensor nodes in order to acquire data and services.

Network Layer. Once the data has been obtained by the sensors, the network layer is responsible for transmitting and processing it. The various solutions proposed at this layer have many advantages. For the problem of encryption, authentication and integrity, the proposed solution is the most secure and effective, consisting of secure end-to-end communication between the Internet and the sensor network [32]. For DDoS attacks in this layer, the solution in [33] is effective for detecting and preventing these attacks, using an algorithm. Being ubiquitous in the IoT environment, human action can also affect the safety of the network. To prevent man-in-the-middle attacks, masquerade attacks and replay attacks, the solution in [37], consisting of using Software Defined Network (SDN)on IoT devices, as a new authentication scheme based on the identity of IoT heterogenous devices.

Middleware Layer. Data recovery and processing is the responsibility of this layer. In [37], to solve the security problem of access control and authentication, the authors proposed a technique for authenticating users on several servers. The scheme is efficient and secure in data transmission. As in [38], the problem of storing data in the Cloud is solved by proposing a lightweight cryptographic algorithm for resource limited devices. This demonstrated the efficiency of the system in processing requests in the database.

Application Layer. It is in the application layer that messages are exchanged between the application and the end users. The various solutions proposed to remedy the problems and attacks provide many advantages in the processing of data transmitted in IoTs. As indicated in [41]; the solution to the problem of access control and authorisation in IoT devices, proposes a framework taking into account access control and authorisation. The proposed framework offers notable flexibility and minimises the communication cost when processing the message exchange. While to solve the inter-device authentication problem and the session key distribution problem, which consists of proposing the IoT-OAS architecture, targeting HTTP/CoAP services. This solution is described as flexible and easy to integrate with external services, with a low processing load and scalable, customisable access. As in [42], the solution to secure communication between objects is to enable inter - device authentication and a session key distribution system. As in [44] the solution to secure communication between objects is to enable inter-device authentication and the session key distribution system. This solution prevents the replay attack, the man-in-the-middle attack, by using the upstream key.

Table 1. XXX.

Layer	Problems/Attacks	Solutions	Advantages/Disadvantages
Perception	-node capture -detection of faulty nodes -theft and destruction of sensors -node reprogramming -Dos attack -communication interception -data cleansing -low sensor power and computing space	-localized fault algorithm -improving PKI -model for a decentralised detection system in WSNs -encryption algorithm -introduction of authentication protocol -Pauthkey plan	-maximum precision and minimum defect rate -low complexity -improves t h e PKI protocol mechanism -prevents disclosure and desynchronization attack
Network	-Replay attack -Dos attack -man-in-the-middle attac -injection attack -DDoS attack	-end-to-end communication mechanism -lightweight algorithm -authentication scheme -mutual authentication architecture -certificate management by IoTssp	-safe and effective -effective for preventing and detecting attacks
Middleware	-big data management difficulty -difficulty filtering valid data -difficulty in managing suspicious data	-cloud solicitation -technique for authenticating users on multiple servers -réduction du temps de communication -encrypted request processing -use of identity and service managers	-efficient and secure data transmission -efficient in handling requests
Application	-bugs -access control, privacy, data leakage -software vulnerability -harpooning -malicious codes -meter/network hacking -security patches and their distribution	-flexible access control and authorization -rchitecture based on the IoT-OAs protocol -authentication between devices and key -use of upstream key to prevent attack	-noticeable flexibility and minimizes the cost of communication -flexible et facile à intégrer -low overhead, scalability, and remote access customization -prevents replay and man-in-the-middle attacks

6.2   Disadvantages of Existing Solutions

The first objective when there is a problem, in any field, is to find solutions. This rule has not escaped the various solutions proposed by different literatures in their quest to pinpoint the attacks and problems that have arisen in the transmission of IoT data. The majority of authors have only described the advantages of their solution, but not its limitations in terms of hardware, software, cost or implementation difficulties. With the exception of [46], the solution to the problem of authenticating data transmitted between the Cloud and intelligent devices, in the middleware layer, which consists of using identity and service managers, is extremely difficult to implement. This type of foresight enables new researchers to find solutions to the limitations of some of these solutions.

7   The Limits of IoT Devices

In order to collect and process information continuously in any environment, IoT devices must be able to resist in terms of energy and also have a large enough storage capacity. Are the various devices used in IoT so far limited? Security in the Internet of Things is crucial, because the privacy of data and users is at stake. Why can't we apply security and make use of the security features of the traditional internet in IoT? In [47], the authors posed the problem of IoT constraints and their effects on the use of cryptographic tools such as those used in the traditional internet. In this study, it was found that there are two main limitations in IoT devices, namely weak batteries and less computing power and memory space, as voluminous data has to be collected and processed continuously.

7.1   Extending Battery Life

To collect information, IoT devices need to be deployed everywhere in any environment. Given that these devices have limited energy (battery), if these resources (of these devices) run out, there will be a discontinuity in the collection or processing of data. This will lead to a breakdown in the functional chain, and therefore a major safety problem. According to [48,52,53], there are three ways of solving this problem. The first is to use minimum security requirements on IoT devices. This solution is not always appreciated, as it may involve also sensitive data. The second proposed solution, which is not also without result is the approach of increasing battery capacity. But the problem is that the majority of IoT devices are designed to be lightweight and small, which blocks the implementation of this solution. Even more complicated in terms of upgrading the hardware and the monetary cost, the third solution consists o f recovering energy from natural resources (for example: heat, vibrations, light, wind, etc.).

7.2   Storage Memory and Light Calculation

In the various literatures consulted, the other problem, and not the least in IoT security, remains the problem of insufficient memory space for data storage and processing. It was noted in [49,54] and [55] that IoT systems cannot work with conventional cryptography for the simple reason that the devices used have very limited memory space and cannot handle the computation and storage requirements of cryptographic algorithms. The authors suggest using existing functions to support security mechanisms on constrained devices. The example evoked in this literature is the authentication of the perception layer by using the signal processing of the receiver side to ensure the origin and location of the transmission (signal of the expected transmitter). Also, according to the same authors, an analog characteristic of a transmitter can be used to efficiently encode analog information. On the other hand, analog nuances cannot be predicted and controlled during the manufacture of IoT devices [50]. The advantage of this authentication technique is that it has little or no energy overhead because it involves radio signals. To solve this data storage problem, [51,56] and [57] propose an algorithm called Encrypted Query Processing for IoT. This technique enables encrypted data to be stored in the cloud with complete security and supports the efficient processing of database queries on this encrypted data.

8   Conclusion

In this survey, we have presented the difference between connected objects and the Internet of Things in two different sections. We have also presented the problem of security in IoTs by examining the various existing literatures, the attacks and problems per layer (perception or physical, network, middleware and application) in the next section. But we have also presented the existing solutions to the various layer attacks in the next section. As with all solutions, in the next section we have reviewed the various advantages and disadvantages still per layer in the IoT, with more advantages than disadvantages, as indicated in the summary table below (Table 1). So, depending on the specific cases, all IoT layers and devices could be vulnerable to certain types of attack. This necessitates a rapid need to think about developing a more general security policy and standards in this new IoT technology. Everyone needs to be involved, whether it's the manufacturing industries or the public sector. IoT device manufacturers and security monitoring agencies work together. Above all, the standards bodies should make it their responsibility to develop solid, robust security standards for IoT devices against new attacks. This survey is expected to serve as a valuable resource for security enhancement for upcoming IoT applications.

References

1. Ding, S., Tukker, A., Ward, H.: Opportunities and risks of internet of things (IoT) technologies for circular business models: a literature review. J. Environm. Manag. **336**, 117662 (2023). ISSN 0301–4797
2. Koohang, A., Sargent, C.S., Nord, J.H., Paliszkiewicz, J.: Internet of Things (IoT): from awareness to continued use. Inter. J. Inform. Manag. 62, 102442 (2022), ISSN 0268–4012

3. Laghari, A.A., Wu, K., Laghari, R.A., et al.: Retracted article: a review and state of art of Internet of Things (IoT). Arch, Comput. Methods Eng. **29**, 1395–1413 (2022)
4. Wang, J., Lim, M.K., Wang, C., Tseng, M.L.: The evolution of the Internet of Things (IoT) over the past 20 years. J. Comput. Indus. Eng. **155**, 107174 (2021). ISSN 0360–8352
5. Noor, M.B.M., Hassan, W.H.: Current research on Internet of Things (IoT) security: a survey. Comput, Netw. **148**, 283–294 (2019), ISSN 1389–1286
6. Schiller, E., Aidoo, A., Fuhrer, J., Stahl, J., Ziorjen, M., Stiller, B.: Landscape of IoT security. Comput. Sci. Rev. **44**, 100467 (2022), ISSN 1574–0137
7. Hassija, V., Chamola, V., Saxena, V., Jain, D., Goyal, P., Sikdar, B.: A survey on IoT Security: application areas, security threats, and solution architectures. IEEE Access **7**, 82721–82743 (2019)
8. Kumar, S., Vidhate, A.: Issues and future trends in IoT security using blockchain: a review. In: 2023 International Conference on Intelligent Data Communication Technologies and Internet of Things (IDCIoT), Bengaluru, India, pp. 976–984 (2023)
9. Lesch, V., Züfle, M., Bauer, A., Iffländer, L., Krupitzer, C., Samuel Kounev, A.: literature review of IoT and CPS-what they are, and what they are not. J. Syst. Softw. **200**, 111631 (2023). https://doi.org/10.1016/j.jss.2023.111631. ISSN: 0164–1212
10. Kaur, B., et al.: Internet of Things (IoT) security dataset evolution: challenges and future directions. Internet of Things **22**, 100780 (2023), ISSN 2542–6605
11. Alsharif, M.H., Jahid, A., Kelechi, A.H., Kannadasan, R.: Green IoT: a review and future research directions. Symmetry **15**, 757 (2023). https://doi.org/10.3390/sym15030757
12. Sadeghi-Niaraki, A.: Internet of Thing (IoT) review of review: bibliometric overview since its foundation. Fut. Generat. Comput. Syst. **143**, 361–377 (2023). https://doi.org/10.1016/j.future.2023.01.016, ISSN 0167–739X
13. Rekha, S., Thirupathi, L., Renikunta, S., Gangula, R.: Study of security issues and solutions in Internet of Things (IoT). Mater. Today: Proc. 80(3), 3554–3559 (2023), ISSN 2214–7853
14. Al-Fuqaha, A., Guizani, M., Mohammadi, M., Aledhari, M., Ayyash, M.: Internet of things: a survey on enabling technologies, protocols, and applications. IEEE Commun. Surv. Tutorials **17**(4), 2347–76 (2015)
15. Yang, Y., Wu, L., Yin, G., Li, L., Zhao, H.: A survey on security and privacy issues in internet-of-things. IEEE Internet Things J. (2017)
16. Borgohain, T., Kumar, U., Sanyal, S.: Survey of security and privacy issues of internet of things. arXiv:1501.02211 (2015)
17. Bouij-Pasquier, I., El Kalam, A.A., Ouahman, A.A., De Montfort, M.: A security framework for Internet of Things. In: Reiter, M., Naccache, D. (eds.) CANS 2015. LNCS, vol. 9476, pp. 19–31. Springer, Cham (2015). https://doi.org/10.1007/978-3-319-26823-1_2
18. Fremantle, P., Scott, P.: A survey of secure middleware for the internet of things. Peer J. Comput. Sci. **3**, e114 (2017)
19. Chen, J., Kher, S., Somani, A.: Distributed fault detection of wireless sensor networks, In: Proceedings of the 2006 Workshop on Dependability Issues in Wireless Ad Hoc Networks and Sensor Networks, pp. 65–72. ACM (2006)
20. Parno, B., Perrig, A., Gligor, V.D.: Distributed detection of node replication attacks in sensor networks. In: IEEE Symposium on Security and Privacy, pp. 49–63. IEEE Computer Society (2005)

21. Wang, X., Gu, W., Schosek, K., Chellappan, S., Xuan, D.: Sensor network configuration under physical attacks. In: Lu, X., Zhao, W. (eds.) ICCNMC 2005. LNCS, vol. 3619, pp. 23–32. Springer, Heidelberg (2005). https://doi.org/10.1007/11534310_5

22. Hartung, C., Balasalle, J., Han, R.: Node compromised in sensor net works: The need for secure systems, Technical Report CU-CS-988-04. University of Colorado at Boulder, Department of Computer Science (2004)

23. Abdul-Ghani,H.A., Konstantas, D., Mahyoub, M.: A comprehensive IoT attacks survey based on a building-blocked reference model. Inter. J. Adv. Comput. Sci. Appli. (ijacsa) **9**(3) (2018)

24. Islam, S.M.R., Kwak, D., Kabir, H., Hossain, M., Kwak, K.-S.: The Internet of Things for health care: a comprehensive survey. IEEE Access **3**, 678–708 (2015)

25. Shemaili, M.B., Yeun, C.Y., Mubarak, K., Zemerly, M.J.: A new lightweight hybrid cryptographic algorithm for the internet of things, pp. 531-534. IEEE (2012)

26. Jing, Q., Vasilakos, A.V., Wan, J., Lu, J., Qiu, D.: Security of the Internet of Things: prospects and changes. Wirel Netw. **20**(8), 2481–2501 (2014)

27. Zhu, S., Setia, S., Jajodia, S.: Leap - efficient security mechanisms for large-scale distributed sensor networks. In: Akyildiz, I.F., Estrin, D., Culler, D.E., Srivas tava, M.B. (eds.) SenSys, pp. 308–309. CMA (2003)

28. Chen, J., Kher, S., Somani, A.: Distributed fault detection of wireless sensor networks. In: Proceedings of the 2006 workshop on reliability issues in wireless ad-hoc networks and sensor networks, DIWANS 2006, pp. 65–72 (2006)

29. Li, C., Raghunathan, A., Jha, N.K.: Insulin pump hijacking: security attacks and defenses for a diabetes treatment system. In: IEEE HealthCom (2011)

30. da Silva, A.P.R., Martins, M.H.T., Rocha, B.P.S., Loureiro, A.A.F., Ruiz, L.B., Wong, H.C.: Decentralized intrusion detection in wireless sensor networks. In: Proceedings of the 1st ACM International Workshop on Amp Security Quality of Service in Wireless and Mobile Networks, Q2SWinet 2005, pp. 16–23 (2005)

31. Wang, Y., Wang, X., Xie, B., Wang, D., Agrawal, D.P.: Intrusion detection in homogeneous and heterogeneous wireless sensor networks. Trans. IEEE Mobile Comput. **7**(6), 698–711 (2008)

32. Aggarwal, R., Das, M.L.: RFID security in the context of the Internet of Things. In: Proceedings of the First International Conference on Internet Security Objects, pp. 51–56. ACM (2012)

33. Gaubatz, G., Kaps, J.P., Ozturk, E., Sunar, B.: State of the art in ultra-low power public key cryptography for wireless sensor networks. In: The third IEEE International Conference on Pervasive Computing and Communications Workshops, pp. 146–150 (March 2005)

34. Huang, S.C.H., Du, D.Z.: New builds on schemas in proceedings of the 24th key predistribution. In: IEEE Joint Annual Conference of Broadcast Encryption Societies of Broadcasting IEEE Computing and Communications Technology, vol 1, pp. 515–523 (March 2005)

35. Chan, H., Perrig, A., Song, D.: Random Key predistribution schemes randomness for sensor networks. In: Symposium 2003 on Security and Privacy 2003, pp. 197–213 (May 2003)

36. A delay-tolerant framework for iot-embeddersns. Comput. Commun. **36**(9) 998–1010 (2013)

37. Liu, H., Bolic, M., Nayak, A., Stojmenovic, I.: Taxonomy and challenges of integrating RFID and wireless sensor networks. IEEE Network **22**(6), 26–35 (2008)

38. Chan, H., Perrig, A.: Pike: intermediate peers for establishing keys in sensor networks. In: IEEE Proceedings 24th Annual Joint Societies Conference 'IEEE Computers and Communications, vol. 1, pp. 524–535 (March 2005)
39. Eschenauer, L., Gligor, V.D.: A key management scheme for distributed sensor networks. In: Proceedings of the 9th ACM Conference on Computer and Information Security, Communications, CCS 2002, pp. 41–47 (2002)
40. Porambage, P., Schmitt, C., Kumar, P., Gurtov, A., Ylianttila, M.: Pauthkey: pervasive authentication protocol and key establishment scheme for networks wireless sensors. Distrib. IoT Appli. International J. Distrib. Sensor Netw. (2014)
41. Raza, S., Duquennoy, S., Chung, T., Yazar, D., Voigt, T., Roedig, U.: Securing communication in 6lowpan withpressed ipsec. In: 2011 International Conference on Distributed Computing in Sensor Systems and Workshops (DCOSS), pp. 1–8 (June 2011)
42. Zhang, C., Green, R.: Communication security in the internet of things: preventive measure and avoidance of DDoS attacks on the IoT network. In: Proceedings of the 18th Communications Symposium and networks, CNS 2015, San Diego, California, USA, Society for Computer Simulation International, pp. 8–15 (2015)
43. Salman, O., Abdallah, S., Elhajj, I.H., Chehab, A., Kayssi, A.: Identity-Based Authentication Scheme for the Internet of Things. In: 2016 IEEE Symposium on Computers and Communication (ISCC), pp. 1109–1111 (June 2016)
44. dos Santos, G.L., Guimaraes, V.T., Cunha Rodrigues, G., Granville, L.Z., Tarouco, L.M.R.: A security architecture based on dtls for the internet Objects. In: 2015 IEEE Symposium on Computers and Communication (ISCC), pp. 809–815 (July 2015)
45. Hummen, R., Ziegeldorf, J.H., Shafagh, H., Raza, S., Wehrle, K.: Towards viable certificate-based authentication for the Internet of Things. In: Proceedings of the 2nd ACM Workshop on Hot Topics in the Wireless Network Security and Privacy, HotWiSec 2013, pp. 37–42 (2013)
46. Tsai, J.L., Nai-Wei, L.: Privacy aware authentication scheme for distributed mobile cloud computing services. J. IEEE Syst. 9(3), 805–815 (2015)
47. Shafagh, H., Hithnawi, A., Droescher, A., Duquennoy, S., Hu, W.: Poster: circa Encrypted Request Processing for the Internet of Things. In: Proceedings of the 21st Annual International Conference on Mobile Computing and Networking, MobiCom 2015, pp. 251–253. ACM, New York (2015)
48. Raza, S., Duquennoy, S., Hoglund, J., Roedig, U., Voigt, T.: Secure communication for the internet of thingsˆaAÿTa comparative of link-layer security and ipsec for 6lowpan. Sec. Commun. Netw. 7(12) (2014)
49. https://www.ibm.com/ca-en/topics/spear-phishing , (Accessed 12 Mar 2023)
50. Seitz, L., Selander, G., Gehrmann, C.: Authorization Framework for the Internet of objects. In: 2013 IEEE 14th International Symposium on a World of Wire less, Mobile and Multimedia Networks (WoWMoM), pp. 1–6 (June 2013)
51. Cirani, S., Picone, M., Gonizzi, P., Veltri, L., Ferrari, G.: Iot-oas: an architecture oauth-based authorization service for secure services in iot scenarios. IEEE Sens. J. 15(2), 1224–1234 (2015)
52. Neisse, R., Steri, G., Baldini, G.: Application of the rules security policy for the internet of things, wireless and mobile computing, networking and communications (WiMob). In: 2014 IEEE 10th International Conference on. IEEE (2014)
53. Park, N., Kang, N.: Mutual authentication scheme in the secure Internet of Things technology for a comfortable lifestyle. Sensors 16(1), 20 (2015), Multidisciplinary Institute of the digital edition

54. Salami, S.A., Baek, J., Salah, K., Damiani, E.: Lightweight encryption for smart home. In: 2016 11th International Conference on Availability, Reliability and Security (ARES), pp. 382–388 (August 2016)
55. Horrow, S., Sardana, A.: Identity management framework for cloud-based internet of things In: First Conference Proceedings International Conference on Internet of Things Security, pp 200–203. ACM (2012)
56. Trappe, W., Howard, R., Moore, R.S.: Low power security: limits and opportunities in the Internet of Things. IEEE Sec. Priv. **13**(1), 14–21 (2015)
57. Yang, Y.C., Wu, L., Yin, G., Li, L., Zhao, H.: A survey of security and privacy issues in the Internet of Things. IEEE Internet of Things J. (2017)

A Location Recommendation Model Based on User Behavior and Sequence Influence

Weixuan Mao[1], Ruwang Wen[1], Zhengxiang Cheng[1], Zhuolin Mei[1,2,3]($\boxtimes$),
Haibin Wang[1], Bin Wu[1,2,3], and Jiaoli Shi[1,2,3]

[1] School of Computer and Big Data Science, Jiujiang, Jiangxi, China
meizhuolin@126.com
[2] Jiujiang Key Laboratory of Network and Information Security, Jiujiang, Jiangxi, China
[3] Institute of Information Security, Jiujiang University, Jiujiang, Jiangxi, China

Abstract. There are evident sequential patterns in human visits to different locations in daily life, which has led to the emergence of numerous sequence-based geographic location recommendation methods. However, previous research has mainly focused on considering the sequential patterns of check-ins as a whole, while overlooking the fact that users' interactive behaviors at check-in locations are likely to influence their preferences for those locations, and subsequently impact their future check-in decisions. The problem of how to fully leverage a user's overall location sequence and location interaction data to provide more personalized recommendations is still unresolved. To address this issue, we propose a geographic location recommendation model called UBSI (User Behavior and Sequence Influence) in this article. Our model is constructed based on check-in sequence, weight model, collaborative filtering, and nth-order additive Markov chain. First, UBSI collects users' check-in sequence and interaction behavior data, generates interest weight using a weight model, integrates personalized data using collaborative filtering method, and finally applies the weighted nth-order additive Markov chain to mine sequential pattern of user check-ins for location recommendations. Finally, we conducted extensive experiments to demonstrate the effectiveness of our approach. The experimental results indicate that our UBSI solution can effectively improve the accuracy of recommendations.

Keywords: Location recommendation · collaborative filtering · interactive behavior · sequence pattern · additive Markov chain

1 Introduction

With the development of mobile devices and geographic positioning technology, the new generation of mobile devices has allowed users to participate in geographic social networks, such as Foursquare, Gowalla, and Brightkite. Users can collect, share, and interact with locations on the geographic social network through handheld devices. By analyzing the interaction data of users at various check-in locations in geographic social networks, their interests and preferences can be understood. This is of great significance for providing personalized location recommendations, as it helps users explore new

K. Ye and L.-J. Zhang (Eds.): ICIOT 2023, LNCS 14208, pp. 18–30, 2024.
https://doi.org/10.1007/978-3-031-51734-1_2

points of interest and can also uncover the implicit relationships between user check-in locations, namely sequence patterns. Based on the fact that human movements exhibit sequential patterns [1, 2], recent studies [3–7] extract sequential patterns from users' check-in location sequence and use them to determine the probability of users visiting new locations given their historical check-in sequence. The specific approach is to extract sequential patterns from the user's check-in sequence using a Markov chain model, and then utilize them to derive the transition probabilities from a check-in location or a sequence of check-in locations to the target location. However, these sequence pattern-based recommendation methods have some limitations. (1) The interaction behavior and sequence effects were not integrated together. These studies did not integrate the sequence effects with the user's interaction behavior data at check-in locations. However, in reality, the user's interactive behaviors such as collecting and sharing are likely to influence their preferences for certain types of locations. Therefore, ignoring these factors may affect the accuracy of the recommendation results. (2) First-order sequence influence. By utilizing the sequence influence based on first-order Markov chains [3–6], efficiency can be improved by considering only the user's most recent visited locations to predict the probability of the user visiting a new location. However, in reality, the predicted probability of visits not only depends on the user's most recent visited locations but also on the locations the user visited earlier. (3) Ignoring the influence of similar locations on the target location. Zhang and Chow et al. developed an efficient nth-order additive Markov chain [7] to predict the visit probability of a user to a new location. By considering all visited locations in the user's check-in history, the model determines the visit probability of the user at a new location. However, in Markov chain models that only consider the type of locations and ignore specific locations, the generation of the matrix overlooks the influence of similar locations on the target location. This oversight may lead to a decrease in the accuracy of the recommendation results.

Based on the above issues, in this article, we propose a weighted location recommendation model called UBSI, which utilizes user check-in sequences and interaction behavior data to address the limitations of current work.

We summarize the contributions of the UBSI model into the following three main aspects:

(1) We have designed a weight model that utilizes user interaction behavior data at check-in locations to calculate the impact of various interaction behaviors on check-in locations and obtain user interest weights for each type of location.
(2) We integrate weight models, collaborative filtering, and nth-order Markov chains together. Firstly, the weight model is used to obtain the user's interest weights for each type of location. Then, collaborative filtering methods are used to filter out the check-in data sets that matches the user's interests. Finally, the recommendation results are processed using the weighted n-order additive Markov chain.
(3) We conducted an experimental evaluation of the recommendation effect of UBSI using a real data sets from Foursquare [8] in a series of experiments. The experimental results indicate that UBSI can provide accurate location recommendations.

The rest of this article is organized as follows. Section 2 focuses on the relevant work. Section 3 introduces background knowledge. In Sect. 4, the specific implementation of the UBSI model is introduced. In Sect. 5, we introduced our experimental setup and analyzed the performance of UBSI. Finally, we summarized this article in Sect. 6.

2 Related Work

In this section, we will focus on discussing the relevant research work conducted in the field of location recommendation in recent years, specifically in the areas of collaborative filtering and sequence influence.

(1) Collaborative filtering technology. The core of collaborative filtering technology is similarity. By finding other users who have similar interests to the target user, items or locations liked by these similar users can be recommended to the target user [9]. Collaborative filtering-based recommendations have been widely applied in various fields such as e-commerce [10], conversation recommendations [11], and article recommendations [12]. For example, in [13], Zhang L et al. believed that different user attributes and quantities of items in the recommendation list have a significant impact on the recommendation results, and proposed an optimized user based collaborative filtering recommendation system. In [14], Wen et al. Provided location recommendation by using a hybrid method of collaborative filtering and Markov chain. Furthermore, some studies have utilized traditional collaborative filtering techniques on user check-in data from GPS trajectory data [15, 16], or text data [17] to provide location recommendations. However, due to the lack of consideration for factors such as the influence of check-in sequence or user interaction behaviors, the personalized recommendation effectiveness of these techniques is quite limited.

(2) Sequence influence. Based on the fact that human movement exhibits sequential patterns [1, 2], sequence techniques are increasingly being used in location recommendation. Now there are various sequence mining techniques [18] available for location prediction. Currently, research on location recommendation using sequence influence can be divided into three groups. (1) Some studies employ data mining techniques to analyze users' travel records and extract the most common location visit sequences as references for travel planning [4]. However, these methods overlook personalized factors, and the sequence patterns they provide do not have distinctiveness for all users. (2) Some studies employ different methods to personalize the modeling of users in order to enhance the personalization level of location sequence pattern. For example, Cheng et al. [3] established a user feature model by analyzing the facial attributes (such as gender and age) implied in the photos shared by users on social platforms. In [19], Kennedy et al. discover aggregated knowledge about geographic areas by analyzing the spatio-temporal patterns of photo tags in those areas. This information is extracted from photos on social platforms. However, compared to location check-in information, the amount of photo data actively uploaded by users on social platforms is relatively low, which also limits the application scope of these methods. (3) The existing majority of works that are based on users' personal location visit sequence extract sequence patterns from check-in location sequences as transition probability matrices and generate location recommendations using Markov chains on these matrices. For example, in [5], Cheng and Yang's research utilizes users' own check-in sequences to establish user features and recommend locations.

However, this method requires users to have over 100 check-in records in order to learn significant sequence patterns, which is not feasible for the majority of users on social platforms who only have a small number of check-in records. In addition, studies [2–4], and [5] have utilized sequence influence based on first-order Markov chain, recommending new locations to users based only on the most recent visited location in their sequences. However, in reality, new locations depend not only on the most recent visited location but also on earlier visited locations. The classical nth-order Markov chain [20] is applied in location recommendation, which considers the dependence of users' possible new access locations on all their historical access locations. However, due to the relatively high time complexity of the classical nth-order Markov chain, it is limited to coarse-grained location recommendation. In [7], Zhang and Chow applied an nth-order additive Markov chain model in location recommendation. Although this model is more efficient than the classical nth-order Markov chain in location recommendation, the matrix generation method in the Markov chain model that considers only the type of locations and ignores specific locations overlooks the influence of locations of the same type on the target location. As a result, the recommendation results are not accurate.

3 Preliminaries

Definition 1: Check-in location sequence and transition. A check-in location sequence of user u is denoted by $P_a = (s_n \rightarrow \cdots s_2 \rightarrow s_1)$. Such that user u visits locations from s_n to s_1 orderly, in which each two-gram subsequence $s_i \rightarrow s_j$ is also called a transition representing u visiting s_i directly before s_j.

Definition 2: General additive Markov chain. Given the user check-in sequence $P_a = (s_n \rightarrow \cdots s_2 \rightarrow s_1)$, the nth-order additive Markov chain generally defines the transition probability of user a visiting a target location after P_a by

$$Pr(s \mid a) = \sum_{i=1}^{n} c(s, s_i, i) \tag{1}$$

where $c(s, s_i, i)$ is the additive contribution of the location s_i to the transition probability $Pr(s \mid a)$.

Definition 3: Importance sampling. Importance sampling is a statistical method used to estimate probability distributions. Specifically, assuming we want to estimate the expected value of a function with respect to a target distribution, we can sample a set of samples from an auxiliary distribution and assign a weight to each sample that reflects the difference between the target distribution and the auxiliary distribution. Then, by multiplying the corresponding weight of the function value for each sample and taking the weighted average, we can obtain an estimate of the expected value of the target distribution.

Definition 4: *Sigmoid* function.
The *Sigmoid* function is often used to map output values to probability values. Its output range is between 0 and 1, which can represent the probability of an event occurring.

The mathematical expression of the *Sigmoid*

$$F(x) = \frac{1}{1 + e^{-x}} \qquad (2)$$

where e is the base of the natural logarithm and x is the input value.

4   Implementation of the UBSI Solution

We introduced the system model of UBSI in Sect. 4.1, the implementation of the weight model in Sect. 4.2, and the specific implementation of the weighted additive Markov chain in Sect. 4.3.

4.1   UBSI System Model

Figure 1 shows an overview of the UBSI model. Firstly, the user's local check-in sequence and interaction behavior with each location are passed to the weighting module, and the interest weight is calculated. Then, based on collaborative filtering methods, data that matches user interests is extracted from the check-in data sets, and a certain amount of data is randomly extracted to ensure user interest expansion. Finally, the aggregated statistical information obtained after processing these data is added to the weighted nth-order additive Markov chain for processing, providing location recommendations for users.

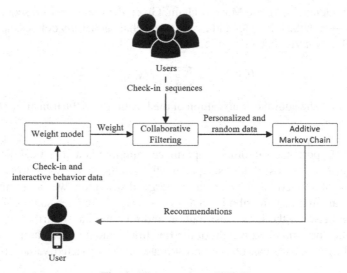

Fig. 1. The overview of UBSI

4.2 Weight Model

We will introduce an overview of the weight model in UBSI, the generation of interest influencing factors, and the generation of interest weight in this section.

Overview of the UBSI Weight Model

Figure 2 shows an overview of the weight model. Firstly, by processing the user's check-in locations and interaction behaviors with that location, a quantitative indicator of interest in that location can be obtained, which we refer to as the interest impact factor b. In order to limit the proportion of interest influence, avoid excessive influence of interest factors, and ensure the expansion of user interest, our model uses function *Sigmoid* (Definition 4) to limit its upper limit, and the quantitative indicator calculated from this is called interest weight β.

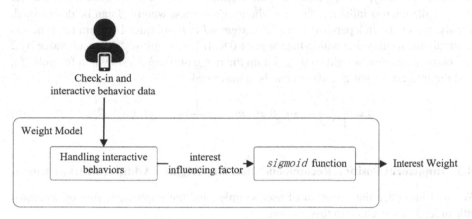

Fig. 2. The Overview of Weight Model

Generation of the Interest Influence Factor

Based on the user's interaction behavior with a certain type of location, we represent the user's collection behavior for a certain location as bs, the sharing behavior as bf, the navigation behavior as bd, the number of check-ins at the location as bq, and the duration of a single visit as bc, as well as the time elapsed since the last visit to the location as be. The user's behaviors of collecting, sharing, navigating, multiple check-ins, and long-term visits to a certain location tend to express the user's preference for the location. However, a long period of time without visiting a certain location may indicate a decrease in the user's interest in the location. Therefore, we assume that the interest influence factor b has a relationship with the above parameters (3).

$$b \propto (bs, bf, bd, bz, bc), b \propto \frac{1}{be} \qquad (3)$$

Let $f(bf, bs, bq, bd)$ represent the weight of behavior, and $g\left(\frac{bc}{be}\right)$ represent the weight of time, By multiplying the behavior weight and time weight, then the value of the interest impact factor b can be calculated (4).

$$b = f(bf, bs, bq, bd) \cdot g\left(\frac{bc}{be}\right) \tag{4}$$

By calculating the interest factor b of the user for each type of location in the local check-in records, the interest influence factor sequence $B_a = (b_n \to \cdots b_2 \to b_1)$ of the local check-in records can be obtained.

Generate Interest Weight
In order to expand the user's interests, an upper limit needs to be added to restrict the interest impact factor, but there is no need to limit the lower limit (the b minimum is 0). Because someone who has never been to a bar may try to go there due to factors such as curiosity or novelty. The *sigmoid* function (Definition 4) is used to standardize the upper limit of the interest influence factor b, the user's interest weight β can be determined. Firstly, we set the independent variable of *sigmoid* to b, subtract 1/2 from the function to obtain the result value within the range of 0 to 1/2, and multiply the result value by 2 to obtain the interest weight value β within the range of $(0,m)$. As shown in formula (5), and the interest weight $\beta \in (0, m)$ can be determined.

$$F(x) = \frac{1}{1 + e^{-x}} \to \beta = 2m \cdot \left(\frac{1}{1 + e^{-b}} - \frac{1}{2}\right), (m \in R) \tag{5}$$

4.3 Implement Position Recommendation for Weighted Additive Markov Chain

We will introduce the selection of user samples and the implementation of weighted nth-order Markov chain in this section.

Determining User Sample Distribution Based on Importance Sampling
Classifying the user check-in trajectories in data sets D can obtain several check-in trajectory sequence data that have been to the same location s as user a, and a new transfer matrix can be calculated from these data. According to the concept of collaborative filtering [9], the results obtained are more in line with user interests.

For example, for the target location s_w, user a_1 calculates the interest weight β_w of user a_1 based on their own interactive behavior data using a weight model. In data sets D, based on location s_w, collaborative filtering methods can be used to filter out k user data samples with check-in positions of all types of s_w. Based on these k check-in trajectory data, a matrix $T_{sw}(s_i \to s_w), (i \le k)$ (hereinafter referred to as T_1) can be generated. Based on the importance sampling concept, the matrix generated in this way also needs to be weighted to determine its influence range. In this article, we take the matrix weight size as $\frac{\beta_w \cdot K}{k}$. The advantages of taking this value are that the weight size of the personalized matrix is directly proportional to the user interest weight, and that when the amount of data k with s_w check-in positions is small, the overall weight of these positions will be set relatively high, ensuring the influence of personalized data on location recommendations. Finally generates a matrix based on weight $\frac{\beta_w \cdot K}{k}$ for user a_1 to personalize the target location s_w. In order to ensure the expansion of users' interests,

$K \cdot (1-\beta)$ user data from all users need to be randomly selected to generate the matrix $T_{no-sw}(s_i \rightarrow s_w)$ (hereinafter referred to as T_2). This ensures that when the interest weight β is 0 or small, that is, there is no interactive behavior data, there is still enough data for location recommendation, and when the β is large, the user's interest can have a greater impact on the final result.

Implementing Weighted Additive Markov Chain
Given the check-in trajectory sequence $P_a = (s_n \rightarrow \cdots s_2 \rightarrow s_1)$ of user a, if the check-in data of target location s and user a have $s = s_i, \forall s_i \in P_a$ (the category of location s and a certain location in the check-in sequence P_a is the same), then based on the user's check-in interaction information, the weight model calculates the corresponding impact factor sequence $B_a = (b_n \rightarrow \cdots b_2 \rightarrow b_1)$, and generates an interest weight β based on the impact factor b for the additive Markov chain, Referring to nth-order additive Markov chains [7], the probability contribution value of local historical check-in interaction information to user a's potential interest in location s can be obtained through formula (6) (Definition 2). Among them, α represents the decay rate, i represents the sequence number of user visits to each location, and the smaller the value i, the closer the corresponding location has been visited. Of note is T_1, generated by users with k data, which includes all k data with s location types in the data sets D. When there are no locations of the same type as the target location in the user's historical check-in record, β is 0. At this time, there is no matrix T_1 generated based on interest weight β, and the recommendation results are completely calculated by matrix T_2.

$$Pr(s \mid a) \propto \sum_{i=1}^{n} 2^{-\alpha i} \cdot \frac{\beta_x \cdot K}{k} \cdot T_1(s_i \rightarrow s), \forall s \in S \tag{6}$$

After applying formula (7), the contribution probability of data sets D towards a user's potential interest in location s is obtained (based on additive Markov chain).Note that T_2 is generated from $[K \cdot (1-\beta_w)]$ randomly selected check-in data sequences from data sets D,This constraint ensures that when β is large, the user's interest can have a significant impact on the final results. It also guarantees that when β is 0 or small, the user can still obtain recommendation results with accuracy not lower than that of the traditional additive Markov chain.

$$Pr(s \mid a) \propto \sum_{i=1}^{n} 2^{-\alpha i} \cdot T_2(s_i \rightarrow s), \forall s \in S \tag{7}$$

Finally, the probability of user A's transfer to the target location is obtained by adding the transfer probabilities P of (6) and (7).When it is necessary to return multiple personalized recommended locations for a user, it can be done by sorting the locations in data sets D based on the $C_s(D)$ value in descending order. The $C_s(D)$ value is determined by the user's historical check-in interaction information $B_a = (b_n \rightarrow \cdots b_2 \rightarrow b_1)$ and historical check-in trajectory information $P_a = (s_n \rightarrow \cdots s_2 \rightarrow s_1)$. The locations with higher $C_s(D)$ values are recommended to the user in descending order, as they are more likely to be of interest to the user.

5 Experimental Results and Analysis

This section introduces experimental evaluation indicators in Sect. 5.1, experimental setup in Sect. 5.2, and experimental results and analysis in Sect. 5.3.

5.1 Evaluation Indicators

In the experiment, we conducted comparative experiments on our UBSI model and the geographic location recommendation model PLORE [7] using traditional nth-order additive Markov chains under evaluation indicators such as precision, recall, and F1-Score.

R_u represents the recommended list of geographical locations calculated by the model based on the user on the training set, while T_u represents the list of geographical locations that the user will actually visit in the future on the test set. The main evaluation methods are:

(1) Precision represents the proportion of the actual number of locations of interest to the recommended number among all predicted results. The calculation formula is as follows:

$$\mathrm{Pr}\,ecision = \frac{\sum\limits_{u \in U} R_u \cap T_u}{\sum\limits_{u \in U} |R_u|}$$

(2) Recall refers to the number of correct recommendations in the recommended results. This method is used to reflect how many geographic locations users will actually go to in the future are predicted by the recommended algorithm. The calculation formula is as follows:

$$\mathrm{Re}call = \frac{\sum\limits_{u \in U} R_u \cap T_u}{\sum\limits_{u \in U} |T_u|}$$

(3) F1 score, also known as balanced score, can be regarded as a weighted average of the precision and recall of the model. The calculation formula is as follows:

$$F1 = \frac{2 * \mathrm{Pr}\,ecision * \mathrm{Re}call}{\mathrm{Pr}\,ecision + \mathrm{Re}call}$$

5.2 Experimental Setup

In the experiment, we used real check-in data from Foursquare [8] from January 2011 to July 2011 as the experimental data sets. The data sets is divided into training and testing sets based on check-in time, rather than using random partitioning methods, because in practice, we can only use past check-in data to predict future check-in events. 80% of the check-in data with earlier timestamps is used as the training set, while another 20% of the check-in data is used as the test set. This experiment was all implemented on an AMD Ryzen7 5800H processor and 16 GB RAM personal computer. However, due to the lack of conditions for calculating more accurate interest weights in experimental data, the interaction behavior of real data sets only temporarily considers the impact of check-in times on a user's interest. The remaining parameters are as follows:

(1) Number of locations accessed by users in the training set (n). N is not adjustable as it is specified by the user.

(2) Number of recommended locations by users (k). We set k to a range of 2 to 20, which is set to 5 by default.

(3) The maximum value of interest weight (m). We set the default value of m to 1, ensuring that interactive behavior has sufficient weight in user interests.

(4) Decay rate (α). We will α Set to the default value of 0.5 in the PLORE [7] experiment, as the decay rate is exponential.

5.3 Experimental Results and Discussion

Experimental Result Comparison. Figures 3, 4, 5, and 6 compare the accuracy of our UBSI model and the PLORE model in terms of the number of recommended locations (k) and the number of user access locations (n) in the training set on foursquare data set.

PLORE. This method [7] is based on the user's check-in sequence and uses the n-order additive Markov chain to mine the user's sequence pattern to achieve location recommendation. However, because it ignores the impact of user interaction behavior on user preferences, its performance is poor.

UBSI. Our proposed UBSI shows better recommended quality in terms of precision, recall rate and F value. Compared with PLORE, it achieves significant improvement. We attribute this to the following two points: (1) the weight of each access location in the user historical check-in sequence is determined by the weight model we designed, which fully considers the impact of user interaction behavior on user preferences. (2) We use the collaborative filtering method to select the data that is more in line with the user's interest as the data set, and give it the appropriate interest weight according to the important sampling idea, making the recommendation more personalized.

Discussion. *The impact of the number of recommended locations on the recommendation effect.* In Figs. 3, 4 and 5, we analyze the impact of the number of recommendations K on the location on the recommendation effect. With the increase of K, the experimental results of UBSI and PLORE are consistent. The recall rate increases gradually, but the precision decreases steadily. The F1 score increases first and then tends to be stable. Under the three measures, the recommendation effect of UBSI is always better than that of PLORE method. The reason for the decrease in precision is that, generally speaking, by returning more locations for users, the system can find more places that users may be interested in visiting. However, since the recommendation technology returns the top k positions with the highest scores, the access probability of the lower ranked positions is low, so the additional recommended positions may not be liked by users. For example, the second returned recommended location has a lower access probability than the first.

The impact of the number of locations users access in the training set. In Fig. 6, we analyze the impact of the number of locations n accessed by users in the training set on the recommendation effect. When users check in more locations, the F1 scores of the two recommended methods increase for a period of time. The reason is that the recommendation system can use more check-in data to more accurately understand the user's preference for location. After the F1 score increases to a certain value, it fluctuates stably within a certain range. However, the F1 score of UBSI method is always higher than that of PLORE method, and has a slow rising trend. This is because when the number of users' sign-in increases, the amount of data of user interaction behavior will also increase. UBSI will further integrate the sequence influence, interaction behavior and weight model based on nth-order additive Markov chain to achieve better performance.

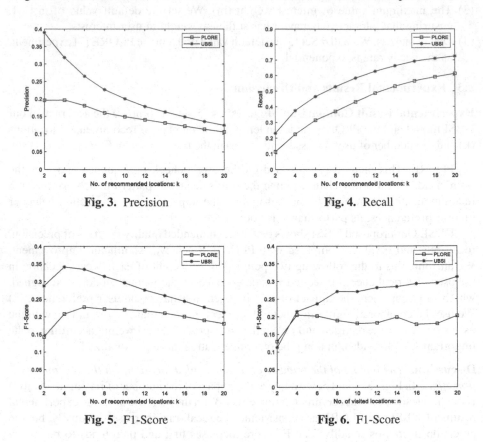

Fig. 3. Precision   **Fig. 4.** Recall

Fig. 5. F1-Score   **Fig. 6.** F1-Score

6   Conclusion

This article proposes a position recommendation system UBSI based on a weight model. Firstly, UBSI utilizes the influence of high-order sequences based on nth-order additive Markov chains. In addition, the impact of each access location on the new location is measured through a weight model, which fully considers the impact of user interaction behavior on user preferences to determine appropriate weights. Simultaneously, collaborative filtering methods are used to filter out data that is more in line with user interests to generate a data sets for recommendation. Finally, experimental results on real-world data sets indicate that UBSI achieves better recommendation performance than position recommendation techniques that only consider the influence of higher-order sequences without considering user interaction behavior.In the future, we plan to expand UBSI and integrate more influencing factors into the weight model to obtain a more personalized location recommendation model.

Acknowledgement. This research is supported by the National Natural Science Foundation of China (No. 61962029, No. 62062045, No. 62262033), the Jiangxi Provincial Natural Science Foundation of China (No. 20202BAB212006) and the Science and Technology Re-search Project of Jiangxi Education Department (No. GJJ201832).

References

1. Cho, E., Myers, S.A., Leskovec, J.: Friendship and mobility: user movement in location-based social networks. In: Proceedings of the 17th ACM SIGKDD International Conference on Knowledge Discovery and Data Mining, pp. 1082–1090 (2011)
2. Gonzalez, M.C., Hidalgo, C.A., Barabasi, A.-L.: Understanding individual human mobility patterns. Nature **453**(7196), 779–782 (2008)
3. Cheng, A.-J., Chen, Y.-Y., Huang, Y.-T., Hsu, W.H., Liao, H.-Y.M.: Personalized travel recommendation by mining people attributes from community-contributed photos. Presented at the Proceedings of the 19th ACM International Conference on Multimedia, Scottsdale, Arizona, USA (2011)
4. Chen, Z., Shen, H.T., Zhou, X.: Discovering popular routes from trajectories. In: 2011 IEEE 27th International Conference on Data Engineering, pp. 900–911. IEEE (2011)
5. Cheng, C., Yang, H., Lyu, M.R., King, I.: Where you like to go next: successive point-of-interest recommendation. In: Twenty-Third International Joint Conference on Artificial Intelligence (2013)
6. Zheng, Y.-T., Zha, Z.-J., Chua, T.-S.: Mining travel patterns from geotagged photos. ACM Trans. Intell. Syst. Technol. (TIST) **3**(3), 1–18 (2012)
7. Zhang, J.-D., Chow, C.-Y., Li, Y.: Lore: exploiting sequential influence for location recommendations. In: Proceedings of the 22nd ACM SIGSPATIAL International Conference on Advances in Geographic Information Systems, pp. 103–112 (2014)
8. Gao, H., Tang, J., Liu, H.: gSCorr: modeling geo-social correlations for new check-ins on location-based social networks. In: Proceedings of the 21st ACM International Conference on Information and Knowledge Management, pp. 1582–1586 (2012)
9. Meng, D.: Collaborative filtering algorithm based on trusted similarity. In: 2018 IEEE 3rd International Conference on Signal and Image Processing (ICSIP), pp. 572–576. IEEE (2018)
10. Zhuang, F., Luo, D., Yuan, N.J., Xie, X., He, Q.: Representation learning with pair-wise constraints for collaborative ranking. In: Proceedings of the Tenth ACM International Conference on Web Search and Data Mining, pp. 567–575 (2017)
11. Chen, Z., et al.: Towards explainable conversational recommendation. In: Proceedings of the Twenty-Ninth International Conference on International Joint Conferences on Artificial Intelligence, pp. 2994–3000 (2021)
12. Nair, A.M., Benny, O., George, J.: Content based scientific article recommendation system using deep learning technique. In: Suma, V., Chen, J.-Z., Baig, Z., Wang, H. (eds.) Inventive Systems and Control. LNNS, vol. 204, pp. 965–977. Springer, Singapore (2021). https://doi.org/10.1007/978-981-16-1395-1_70
13. Zhang, L., Liu, X., Cao, Y., Wu, B.: O-recommend: an optimized user-based collaborative filtering recommendation system. In: 2018 IEEE 24th International Conference on Parallel and Distributed Systems (ICPADS), pp. 212–219. IEEE (2018)
14. Wen, R., Cheng, Z., Mao, W., Mei, Z., Shi, J., Cheng, X.: HMGR: a hybrid model for geolocation recommendation. In: Zhang, S., Hu, B., Zhang, L.J. (eds.) BigData 2023. LNCS, vol. 14203, pp. 48–62. Springer, Cham (2023). https://doi.org/10.1007/978-3-031-44725-9_4

15. Leung, K.W.-T., Lee, D.L., Lee, W.-C.: CLR: a collaborative location recommendation framework based on co-clustering. In: Proceedings of the 34th International ACM SIGIR Conference on Research and Development in Information Retrieval, pp. 305–314 (2011)
16. Zheng, V.W., Zheng, Y., Xie, X., Yang, Q.: Towards mobile intelligence: learning from GPS history data for collaborative recommendation. Artif. Intell. **184**, 17–37 (2012)
17. Hu, B., Ester, M.: Spatial topic modeling in online social media for location recommendation. In: Proceedings of the 7th ACM Conference on Recommender Systems, pp. 25–32 (2013)
18. Ying, J.J.-C., Lee, W.-C., Weng, T.-C., Tseng, V.S.: Semantic trajectory mining for location prediction. In: Proceedings of the 19th ACM SIGSPATIAL International Conference on Advances in Geographic Information Systems, pp. 34–43 (2011)
19. Kennedy, L., Naaman, M., Ahern, S., Nair, R., Rattenbury, T.: How flickr helps us make sense of the world: context and content in community-contributed media collections. In: Proceedings of the 15th ACM International Conference on Multimedia, pp. 631–640 (2007)
20. Zhang, J.D., Ghinita, G., Chow, C.Y.: Differentially private location recommendations in geosocial networks. In: 2014 IEEE 15th International Conference on Mobile Data Management, vol. 1, pp. 59–68. IEEE (2014)

GPChain: Optimizing Cross-Shard Transactions and Load Imbalance in Sharded Blockchain Networks

Hongmu Han[1]($\boxtimes$), Sheng Chen[1], Zhigang Xu[1], Xinhua Dong[1], and Wenlong Tian[2]

[1] School of Computer Science, Hubei University of Technology, Wuhan 430068, China
hanhongmu@hbut.edu.cn
[2] School of Computer, University of South China, Hengyang 421001, China

Abstract. Sharded blockchain provides a better linear scalability and scalability compared to traditional blockchain by dividing the blockchain into several disjoint shards, making it a more suitable blockchain solution for the Internet of Things (IoT). However, the transaction data generated by devices in the network also follows a power-law distribution, resulting in a large number of cross-shard transactions and shard load imbalance due to popular addresses when partitioning transactions into shards. Moreover, the atomicity of transactions requires cross-shard transactions to wait for confirmation from multiple shards, further prolonging the confirmation time due to transaction congestion in shards. In this paper, we propose GPChain (Graph Partitioning Chain), a graph-based sharding blockchain transaction optimization scheme. We address the challenges of load imbalance in shards caused by power-law distribution and excessive cross-shard transactions through an enhanced graph partitioning algorithm. Experimental results demonstrate that GPChain outperforms other solutions in terms of cross-shard transaction ratio and shard load balancing.

Keywords: Blockchain · Sharding · Graph Partitioning · Community Detection

1 Introduction

With the rapid development of Internet of Things (IoT) technology, the number of devices connected to the network is experiencing explosive growth. However, existing solutions struggle to meet the increasing demands of device and network scale, leaving devices vulnerable during communication and storage processes. Blockchain technology, with its decentralized, tamper-resistant, and traceable features, is naturally suited for distributed environments in the IoT. However, blockchain technology also has its drawbacks, such as low transaction processing efficiency and scalability, which must be addressed before widespread adoption in large-scale applications.

In order to enhance the transaction processing performance and scalability of blockchain, researchers have proposed sharding schemes based on the concept

K. Ye and L.-J. Zhang (Eds.): ICIOT 2023, LNCS 14208, pp. 31–46, 2024.
https://doi.org/10.1007/978-3-031-51734-1_3

of database sharding. By employing different organizational methods [11], the original blockchain is divided into disjoint shards, thereby reducing the storage pressure on the ledger and enabling parallel processing of transactions. Despite the ability of sharding to enable parallel processing of transactions across multiple shards, the problem of hot shard still exists in practice [10]. This phenomenon arises due to the power-law distribution observed in transactions, whereby popular addresses, such as those associated with exchanges, receive a higher volume of transaction requests compared to regular personal account addresses within a given time period. When accounts from other shards need to transact with the address belonging to the hotspot shard, the transaction requires confirmation from both the source and target shards, as the transaction typically occurs across multiple shards. As a result, the shard containing the popular address becomes congested [21]. In this paper, we focus on utilizing graph partitioning to address the following issues caused by power-law distribution in blockchain transaction graph data.

Shards Load Balancing Problem: To ensure the security of transactions within shards, existing approaches go beyond solving hash puzzles by combing them with random assignment strategies. The intention is to prevent nodes from knowing in advance which shard they will be assigned to. This approach aims to evenly distribute malicious nodes across shards as much as possible. However, account addresses are randomly allocated to different shards for security purposes, leading to a significant disparity in the number of transactions generated by different accounts within each shard. For example, the transactions associated with the top-tier cryptocurrency exchange Binance on the Ethereum blockchain account for 2% of the overall user base [11]. Shards containing clusters of popular account addresses may generate tens of thousands of transactions within a short period, while shards without these popular addresses may only generate and store a minimal amount of transaction data. Consequently, the random allocation of accounts exacerbates the imbalance in the workload between shards, making resource scheduling and allocation more challenging.

Cross-Shard Transaction Blocking Problem: In a state sharding, each shard holds its independent shard state data. This means that when a transaction involves accounts from multiple shards, the transaction needs to be confirmed by multiple shards. If multiple shards need to perform cross-shard transactions with the same shard, a large number of transactions can block that shard, resulting in an infinite extension of transaction confirmation time. Due to the presence of Preferential Attachment, the shard where Binance addresses are located receives transaction requests from 2% of all accounts. These accounts are more likely to be distributed across other shards. When conducting cross-shard transactions with the shard where Binance is located, they require confirmation from that shard, resulting in a lack of parallel confirmation. Therefore, the preferential attachment caused by power law distribution leads to cross-shard transaction blocking, ultimately reducing the effective throughput of sharding blockchain.

To address these challenges, we propose a novel sharded blockchain protocol scheme that tackles the load balancing problem between shards while minimizing cross-shard transactions. This problem is known to be NP-hard and poses significant practical implementation challenges for state sharding mechanisms. Our approach transforms transactions into a graph partitioning problem and partitions the graph edges to achieve workload balance across all shards [20]. The main contributions of our scheme are summarized below.

- We transform the challenges of cross-shard transactions and load imbalance in blockchain into a graph partitioning problem. With the proposed graph partitioning algorithm, we achieve better balance graph partitioning results for power-law graphs through vertex cuts.
- We propose a state sharding optimization scheme by combining the graph partationing algorithm. This scheme involves reassigning and reconfiguring the state tree of node accounts to reduce the preferential attachment between highly connected nodes and low-degree nodes in the graph caused by power-law distributions, thereby reducing cross-shard transactions.
- Through comprehensive experimental verification using Ethereum transaction data, the proposed sharding scheme can significantly reduce the number of cross-shard transactions compared to Brokerchain's sharding scheme.

2 Background and Related Work

2.1 Blockchain Sharding

Currently, researchers have proposed numerous sharding solutions to enhance the scalability of blockchain systems. In Monoxide [14], a new relay transaction mechanism is utilized to handle cross-shard transactions. Huang et al. [5] propose a state sharding protocol called brokerchain, which achieves load balancing between shards by dividing states and relaying transactions through brokers. Xi et al. [15] introduce a dynamic sharding scheme based on a Hidden Markov Model, enabling adaptive updates of shards through finer-grained partitioning. Xu et al. [17] propose a clustering-based non-exhaustive genetic algorithm to solve the sharding problem. Articles [3,7,18] optimize blockchain sharding using deep learning techniques to achieve better performance. Cai et al. [1] present a solution named Benzene, which reduces cross-shard communication and storage overhead through a Trusted Execution Environment (TEE) and a dual-chain collaborative architecture. Existing solutions tend to focus on solving the scalability problem of sharding through machine learning methods while overlooking the underlying causes of the sharding problem.

2.2 Balanced Graph Partitioning

The goal of balanced graph partitioning is to simultaneously achieve load balancing and minimize communication costs. However, this problem has been proven to be NP-hard, making it challenging to find the optimal solution within a limited time frame. Based on the running process of algorithms, graph partitioning algorithms can be classified into static graph partitioning and dynamic graph partitioning. Static graph partitioning algorithms typically use spectral methods, heuristic methods, or multi-level partitioning methods to partition static graph data. For example, the classic algorithm Metis [8] adopts a multi-level partitioning strategy. In addition, other static methods such as NE [20] and PowerLyra [2] partition graphs using different approaches like vertex cut and mixed cut compared to Metis. On the other hand, dynamic graph partitioning, also known as streaming graph partitioning algorithms, such as Greedy [4], Grid [6], and HDRF [12], only require reading one edge (or vertex) at a time. However, compared to static partitioning methods, they typically have weaker accuracy in terms of runtime. Both approaches have their advantages in different types of graph data. Existing research has shown that for power-law distributed data, vertex cut has better performance compared to edge cut [12,16].

2.3   Cross-Shard Transaction

In sharded blockchains, where each shard does not have the complete state, it is necessary to consider how to maintain the atomicity of transactions when dealing with cross-shard transactions. In Omniledger [9], the authors adopt a client-driven two-phase commit (2PC) mechanism with lock/unlock operations to ensure the atomicity of cross-shard transactions. RapidChain [19] achieves atomicity by routing all involved UTXOs to the same shard, thereby transforming cross-shard transactions into intra-shard transactions. In Monoxide [14], deduction and deposit operations are performed separately, and a relay transaction mechanism is used to achieve final atomicity for cross-shard transactions. Brokerchain [5] employs intermediary nodes called brokers to act as relays and guarantors for cross-shard transactions. In the S-store scheme [13], the authors propose using consistent hashing to reduce data migration between shards based on an Aggregate Merkle B+ (ABM) tree. It can be observed that existing solutions often focus on ensuring the consistency of transactions between the two shards involved, starting from the transactions, but lack attention to the accounts of the two parties involved.

3   Overview of GPChain

In this section, we will describe how GPChain works. As a sharding solution that focuses on addressing load balancing and cross-shard transaction issues between shards, this paper solves the transaction imbalance caused by random node allocation and the power-law distribution of transactions by partitioning the transaction state graph. Security is not the main focus of this research, so the proposed solution is designed based on a permissioned blockchain. The symbols used in this article are shown in Table 1, Similar to most state sharding approaches, we define an epoch as a fixed period in which the blockchain operates, and perform consensus and account reconfiguration processes on an epoch basis. All shards have the same structure and run the PBFT consensus protocol to handle shard transactions. The protocol performs transaction packing and consensus during the consensus period, and performs partitioning of the account state graph and reaches consensus on the result during the account reconfiguration period. The proposed solution is illustrated in Fig. 1, and the three main stages of the process are described as follows:

Table 1. Symbols and Notations.

Symbol	Notation
v	Vertex of account
e	Edge of transaction
$G(v, e)$	Transaction state graph
$G^{'}(v, e)$	Weighted transaction state graph
P_{Shard}	Primary Node of shard
P_{Leader}	Primary Node of all shard

Transaction State Graph Generation Phase: During the account reconfiguration period of each epoch, the last round's primary node, P_{Shard}, who successfully achieved PBFT consensus within each shard, acts as the primary node for that shard. P_{Shard} is responsible for collecting the transactions within the shard for that round and generating the sub-transaction state graph $G^{'}(v, e)$ for that shard. Here, v is defined as the account address, and e is defined as a transaction between two accounts. Subsequently, the Raft protocol selects a leader node, P_{Leader}, among all the shards' P_{Shard} nodes. The shard where P_{Leader} is located is responsible for collecting the sub-transaction state graphs $G^{'}(v, e)$ from each shard and generating the weighted undirected global state graph $G(v, e)$ for that epoch.

State Graph Partitioning Phase: The shard where P_{Leader} is located is responsible for the state graph partitioning. P_{Leader} first loads the generated weighted undirected state graph and runs a vertex cut algorithm based on community detection to partition transactions into different partitions, each representing a blockchain shard. Subsequently, the partitioning result for each account is determined based on the transactions it is associated with and the partition it belongs to. When a transaction associated with an account exists in multiple shards, account copies are created to achieve state synchronization for the account across multiple shards.

State Reconfiguration Phase: After obtaining the state graph partitioning result, P_{Leader} broadcasts the partitioning result to other shards and achieves consensus on the result using the Raft protocol. Each shard configures the account information within the shard based on the partitioned state graph. When a new round of transactions begins, the transactions are allocated to the designated shard for processing.

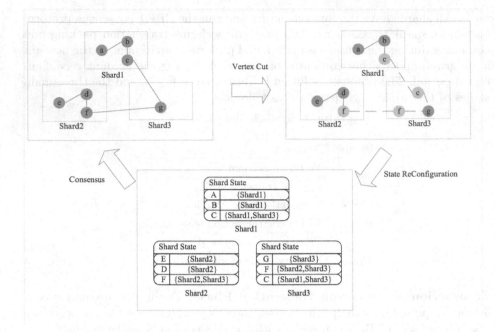

Fig. 1. Process of GPChain.

4   Protocol Design

To address the challenge of high cross-shard transaction volume after state sharding, this section proposes a novel blockchain sharding scheme. Specifically, we
first use a community detection based graph partitioning to partition the transaction data's state graph in order to reduce the generation of cross-shard transactions. Then, we utilize a more granular shard state tree to build a state synchronization scheme to achieve consistency of account states across shards. Finally,
the blockchain will confirm new transactions based on the reconfigured account
state.

4.1   Community-Based Graph Partitioning

In existing state sharding blockchains, the process of allocating nodes to shards is
often independent of the attributes of the nodes themselves, such as their degree
information, which typically represents the number of other nodes they transact with. Considering the relationships between nodes, community detection is
a feasible method that can aggregate nodes v in graph G into several communities based on modularity. The resulting aggregation often leads to stronger
connectivity within communities and weaker connectivity between communities.
The Louvain algorithm [8] is a typical community detection algorithm that is
used to identify the distribution of communities in transaction graphs, grouping

nodes with more shared characteristics into the same community. When applying it to blockchain transaction graphs, our objective is to minimize cross-shard
transactions by finding the same community of addresses that have more common transaction counterparts. Although Louvain seems capable of achieving this
goal, it partitions the nodes represented by account addresses, whereas our goal
is to partition communities based on the edges represented by transactions. Previous work has shown that vertex-cut algorithms perform better than edge-cut
algorithms when dealing with power-law distributed data. Therefore, by combining the degree relationships of nodes with the community relationships of
Louvain, we design a greedy algorithm based on vertex cutting. When applied
to partition power-law distributed blockchain state graphs, this algorithm can
partition the edges associated with transactions into communities within a finite
time, as shown in Algorithm 1.

Algorithm 1: Community detection

Input: G_e : A set of transactions in epoch ;
N : number of shards
Output: C_{Tx} : Community of TX
1 **Function** *community detection(G_e,N)*:
2    $C \leftarrow Louvain(G_e)$
3   ; $C' \leftarrow$ Vector2Edge(C, G_e)
4   ; $Avg_c = $ total$(G_e) \div N$ //Calculate the number of edge in G
5   ; **foreach** $c \in C'$ **do**
6   **if** *sum(c > Avg_c)* **then**
7        $C_{Tx} \leftarrow$ HDRF$(c,$total$(G_e) \div Avg_c)$
8   ; //Dividing Large Communities through HDRF
9   **else**
10        $C_{Tx} \leftarrow c$
11   **end**
12   **end**
13   **return** C_{Tx}
14 **end**
15 **Function** *Vector2edge(C, G_e)*:
16   **foreach** $Tx \in G_e$ **do**
17   **if** *Two accounts belong to the same community* **then**
18   Tx is divided into this community
19   **else**
20   Tx is divided into smaller communities
21   **end**
22   **end**
23   **return** C' //Convert Vector Community to Edge Community
24 **end**

In our proposed solution, we first use the Louvain algorithm to assign communities to each vertex. Then, we traverse every transaction in graph G and pri-

oritize assigning the transaction to the community of the node with lower degree among the transaction participants. This approach aims to minimize the replication factor in vertex-cut, ensuring that high-degree vertexs have fewer copies. Additionally, to prevent excessively large communities, we employ the HDRF algorithm to trim oversized communities and divide them into appropriate sizes. The HDRF algorithm is specifically designed for power-law distributions and performs well in datasets with highly connected vertices. By applying these steps, we partition transactions into communities of varying sizes, reducing communication overhead between communities. However, we still need to distribute the communities across multiple shards to complete our hybrid-cut algorithm. The greedy method is a commonly used heuristic algorithm that offers good accuracy and low computational cost. Therefore, we use it to allocate communities of edge sets to shards, as outlined in Algorithm 2.

Algorithm 2: Greedy partition

Input: C_{Tx} : Community of TX ;
N : number of shards
Output: N_i : set shard n of vector i
1 **Function** $greedy\ partition(C_{Tx},N)$:
2     $C' \leftarrow \text{Sort}(C_{Tx})$
3   ; **foreach** $c \in C'$ **do**
4   minLoadShard $\leftarrow c$
5   ; // Allocate edge set c to the minimum load shard
6   **end**
7     $AvgLoad = totalLoad \div N$
8   ; $diff = maxLoad - minLoad$
9   ; **while** $diff > AvgLoad$ **do**
10        $c_{min} \in maxLoad$
11   ; $minLoad \leftarrow c_{min}$
12   ; $diff = maxLoad - minLoad$
13   ; //Move the smallest community in maxLoad to minLoad
14   **end**
15   **return** N_i
16 **end**

Similar to common greedy methods, we sort the communities based on the number of edges and then distribute them into several shards to minimize the imbalance in shard sizes. This approach aims to achieve load balancing between shards. In the end, we can easily determine the shards to which each account is assigned based on the transactions that are partitioned into each shard.

4.2 Account Status Reconfiguration

After the accounts within a single shard are partitioned into multiple accounts, their states across multiple shards need to be synchronized in some way.In

Ethereum, there are four main tree structures: the world state tree, the transaction tree, the receipt tree, and the smart contract account tree, with the smart contract account tree stored in the leaf vertexs of the world state tree. The world state tree is responsible for maintaining account information, mapping account addresses to their respective states. The transaction tree and receipt tree store the transactions and receipts of a block, respectively. The smart contract account tree stores information related to smart contracts. In a state sharding blockchain, due to the absence of cross-shard states between shards, individual shard state trees cannot directly store the states of vertexs in other shards. Additionally, each shard block requires a state tree as the root hash of the state, making it impractical for all shards to collectively store the world state tree. Therefore, we choose to allow each shard to construct its own shard state tree. The state tree still maintains the mapping of accounts to addresses, but with the addition of a mapping to indicate the shard where each account belongs, as shown in Fig. 2.

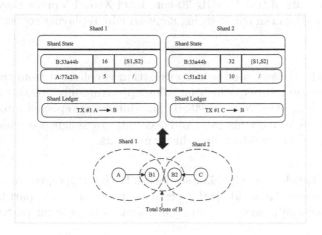

Fig. 2. Mapping account addresses to multiple shards

For example, when account B is assigned to shards shard1 and shard2, both shard1 and shard2 will have the state tree leaf vertex for account B. The state trees in the two shards will respectively maintain the balances B1 and B2 for account B within each shard. Transactions within a shard will only consume the balances within that shard. When querying the total balance of account B, it can be obtained by querying the list of shards where account B is located. Although it may seem like account B has been divided into two accounts, the shard allocation list maintained for each account b in each shard can easily retrieve the state of account B from all the shards it belongs to, thus obtaining the final global state. After the account is partitioned, it is necessary to allocate the balance owned by each account in each shard. If the balance is simply evenly distributed among each shard, it may result in some shards running out of account balances earlier due to different numbers of transactions within each shard. Therefore, the allocation of account balances is determined by the following formula 1

$$V_i = \frac{Tx_i}{Tx_{total}} \times V_{total} \qquad\qquad (1)$$

In the formula, V_i represents the balance of the current shard after the partition, Tx_i represents the transaction volume within the shard during that round of partitioning, Tx_{total} represents the total transaction volume related to the account, and V_{total} represents the total balance of the account.

5   Evaluation

5.1   Environment and Settings

Experimental Prototype: To evaluate the proposed GPChain, we implemented a sharding simulator based on Python and deployed it on a local server. The server consists of two 2.4 GHz 20-core Intel Xeon E5 processors and 32 GB of memory. We then ran our sharding simulator by replaying collected historical transactions.

Data Set: The dataset used in our evaluation is collected from the Ethereum public transaction dataset, which includes approximately 500,000 transactions from block height 5181526 to 5184886. The dataset is replayed into the experimental prototype at a certain rate, and accounts are assigned to different shards based on their respective baseline scheme methods.

BaseLine: Consider three baseline scenarios: HDRF [12] represents a dynamical vertex cut scheme, Monoxide [14] represents a random node partition scheme, and Brokerchain [5] represents a edge cut followed by account partitioning approach.

Metrics: We first compared our proposed node cut algorithm with existing vertex cut algorithms in terms of replication factor, Load standard deviation, and runtime. The replication factor represents the ratio of the number of nodes in the partitioned graph to the original number of nodes, which measures the size of the cut nodes and potential communication costs. The Load standard deviation is used to measure the relative standard deviation of the number of edges in each partition after partitioning. The closer it is to 0, the closer the number of edges in each partition is. Furthermore, we compared the TX throughput, cross-shard transaction ratio, and partition load of GPChain with other baseline schemes.

5.2   Experimental

We first compare the hybrid-cut scheme proposed in this paper with HDRF, a algorithm specifically designed for power-law distributions, based on 100,000, 300,000, and 500,000 transactions. We calculate the replication factor, relative standard deviation of the load, and runtime for each case, and the results are shown in Fig. 3, 4 and 5: From Fig. 3 and 4, it can be observed that as the number of transactions increases, the replication factor and the standard deviation of partition load also increase. The improved hybrid-cut algorithm, which preserves the community relationships between accounts, performs better with smaller partitions, while HDRF maintains a relatively stable replication factor across different partition sizes. In terms of load standard deviation, HDRF's greedy rule prioritizes partitioning strategies that reduce the replication factor. However, when there are a large number of duplicate transactions, the penalty term cannot balance the partition load and replication factor. In contrast, the proposed solution in this paper, based on the secondary partitioning of communities, can more effectively balance multiple partitions.

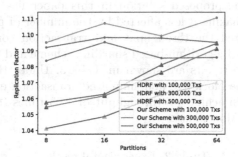

Fig. 3. Replication Factor of two schemes under 100,000,300,000, and 500,000 Txs

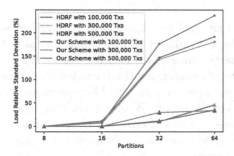

Fig. 4. Load standard deviation of two schemes under 100,000,300,000, and 500,000 Txs

Figure 5 illustrates the difference in running time between the two algorithms. It can be observed that HDRF's runtime efficiency depends on the number of partitions and the number of transactions, as it needs to calculate the score for each transaction with respect to each partition. On the other hand, the main

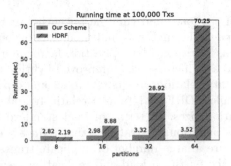

Fig. 5. runtime of two schemes

time overhead of the proposed solution in this paper lies in the community partitioning stage, making it less affected by the number of partitions.

We then compared the throughput and transaction confirmation latency between the improved algorithm-based sharding scheme and the existing sharding scheme, and the results are shown in Table 3. Under the condition of 32 shards with the same block size and simulated transaction environment within each shard, GPChain achieves a throughput of 1.05 times that of Brokerchain and 2 times that of Monoxide.

Table 2. Experimental results.

Schemes	Monoxide	Brokerchain	GPChain
Avg.Systemthroughput(TPS)	146	284	298

Afterwards, we partitioned the dataset into a training set and a testing set based on the chronological order of transactions. By using the training set, we obtained the graph partitioning of transaction states. Then, we replayed a portion of the testing set data containing the partition states into the blockchain to obtain more detailed data between shards. The results are shown below. Figure 6 presents a comparison of the proposed solution in this paper with existing sharding blockchain solutions in terms of cross-shard transaction rate. Monoxide represents a scheme where nodes are randomly assigned to shards, Metis utilizes the point-cut method to reassign nodes, Brokerchain partitions a portion of accounts based on Metis, and our approach applies the hybrid-cut method to partition accounts.

It can be observed that all methods show an improvement in cross-shard transaction rate as the number of partitions increases. Random partitioning and Metis-based Edge-cut optimization are more affected by the number of partitions, while Brokerchain, which partitions based on edges, and our proposed solution are less affected and demonstrate lower cross-shard transaction rates at various partition sizes.

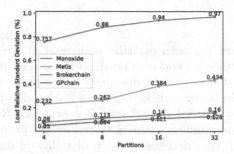

Fig. 6. Cross-Shard Txs ratio for Different Schemes

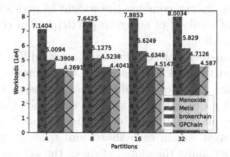

Fig. 7. Total load of shards for Different Schemes

Figure 7 and Table 2 respectively illustrate the overall load of the blockchain and a more detailed load analysis under different numbers of shards. It can be observed that Monoxide's random partitioning achieves a better average load per shard, but the total load increases due to the atomicity requirement of cross-shard transactions. Metis and Brokerchain, although having a smaller total load, exhibit a significant imbalance in load between shards. On the other hand, the proposed solution in this paper achieves better results in terms of both average load and load imbalance between shards.

Table 3. Experimental results.

Partitions	8			16			32			64		
	Max	Min	Avg	Max	Min	Avg	Max	Min	Avg	Max	Min	Avg
Monoxide	18514	17017	17851	11769	8134	9553	7399	3401	4928	4445	1535	2501
Metis	24100	7689	12523	14329	3470	6409	6888	1372	3515	4585	275	1821
Brokerchain	22725	5401	10977	13141	2424	5654	6691	708	2896	4313	58	1472
GPChain	12483	9608	10672	6745	4137	5505	4357	1519	2821	2449	559	1433

6 Discussion

The issue of Hot shard has been partially addressed in the proposed solution. However, there are still some concerns (such as shard security and data consistency across shards) that need to be discussed before application.

The problem of clustering malicious nodes within a shard is also challenging to address in existing sharded blockchains. For example, Rapidchain [19] and Monoxide [14] often use random sharding to reduce the proportion of malicious nodes within a shard, thus decreasing the probability of malicious nodes controlling a shard. In our solution, in order to achieve the goal of balanced graph partitioning, it is not feasible to perform a secondary random sharding on all nodes. To address this, we can combine the weight of nodes within a shard with the random election of a subset of nodes to participate in consensus to enhance the security of our sharding.

Regarding the consistency of account data across different shards, although some accounts are partitioned and assigned to different shards, each shard records the intra-shard transaction information between the shard and that account. By aggregating the legitimate states within each shard, the global state of the account in the blockchain can be obtained, and its global reliability is ensured by the consensus within each shard and the security of blocks. When each shard operates normally, the global state of the account can be obtained.

7 Conclusion

The introduction of sharding has provided blockchain with higher system throughput, but it has also brought new challenges. In this paper, we explain the reasons behind the overheating of blockchain sharding, which is the imbalance caused by preferential attachment of account addresses, leading to transaction blocking across multiple shards. We propose a vertex-cut algorithm for the transaction state graph of power law distributed blockchain, based on community detection, to optimize cross-shard transactions in sharded blockchains. By dividing the transaction state graph of sub-shards into communities and then partitioning the vertexs based on community association, we achieve the partitioning of high-degree vertex accounts. Through the account synchronization mechanism across shards, we achieve load balancing among shards. Experimental evaluations have shown that our proposed approach can effectively reduce the proportion of cross-shard transactions and the overall load on shards in sharded blockchains compared to existing solutions. Additionally, the more fine-grained account partitioning strategy can effectively reduce network centralization caused by nodes with strong computing power. In future work, we will focus on researching the relationship between security within shards and account reconfiguration.

Acknowledgments. This work is supported by the Key-Area Research and Development Program of Hubei Province 2022BAA040, the Science and Technology Project of Department of Transport of Hubei Province 2022-11-4-3, and the Innovation Fund of

Hubei University of Technology BSQD2019027, BSQD2019020 and BSQD2016019. We sincerely thank the anonymous reviewers for their very comprehensive and constructive comments.

References

1. Cai, Z., et al.: Benzene: scaling blockchain with cooperation-based sharding. IEEE Trans. Parallel Distrib. Syst. **34**(2), 639–654 (2023). https://doi.org/10.1109/ TPDS.2022.3227198
2. Chen, R., Shi, J., Chen, Y., Zang, B., Guan, H., Chen, H.: PowerLyra: differentiated graph computation and partitioning on skewed graphs. ACM Trans. Parallel Comput. **5**(3), 13:1–13:39 (2018). https://doi.org/10.1145/3298989
3. Gao, N., Huo, R., Wang, S., Huang, T., Liu, Y.: Sharding-Hashgraph: a high-performance blockchain-based framework for industrial internet of things with hashgraph mechanism. IEEE Internet Things J. **9**(18), 17070–17079 (2022). https://doi.org/10.1109/JIOT.2021.3126895
4. Gonzalez, J.E., Low, Y., Gu, H., Bickson, D., Guestrin, C.: PowerGraph: distributed graph-parallel computation on natural graphs (2012). https://www. usenix.org/conference/osdi12/technical-sessions/presentation/gonzalez
5. Huang, H., Peng, X., Zhan, J., Zhang, S., Lin, Y., Zheng, Z., Guo, S.: Brokerchain: A cross-shard blockchain protocol for account/balance-based state sharding (2022). https://doi.org/10.1109/INFOCOM48880.2022.9796859
6. Jain, N., Liao, G., Willke, T.L.: GraphBuilder: scalable graph ETL framework (2013). https://doi.org/10.1145/2484425.2484429, https://event.cwi.nl/ grades2013/04-jain.pdf
7. Jia, D., Xin, J., Wang, Z., Wang, G.: Optimized data storage method for sharding-based blockchain. IEEE Access **9**, 67890–67900 (2021). https://doi.org/10.1109/ ACCESS.2021.3077650
8. Karypis, G., Kumar, V.: A fast and high quality multilevel scheme for partitioning irregular graphs. SIAM J. Sci. Comput. **20**(1), 359–392 (1998). https://doi.org/ 10.1137/S1064827595287997
9. Kokoris-Kogias, E., Jovanovic, P., Gasser, L., Gailly, N., Syta, E., Ford, B.: OmniLedger: a secure, scale-out, decentralized ledger via sharding (2018). https:// doi.org/10.1109/SP.2018.000-5
10. Li, Y., Wang, J., Zhang, H.: A survey of state-of-the-art sharding blockchains: models, components, and attack surfaces. J. Netw. Comput. Appl. **217**, 103686 (2023). https://doi.org/10.1016/j.jnca.2023.103686
11. Luu, L., Narayanan, V., Zheng, C., Baweja, K., Gilbert, S., Saxena, P.: A secure sharding protocol for open blockchains (2016). https://doi.org/10.1145/2976749. 2978389
12. Petroni, F., Querzoni, L., Daudjee, K., Kamali, S., Iacoboni, G.: HDRF: stream-based partitioning for power-law graphs (2015). https://doi.org/10.1145/2806416. 2806424
13. Qi, X.: S-store: a scalable data store towards permissioned blockchain sharding (2022). https://doi.org/10.1109/INFOCOM48880.2022.9796800
14. Wang, J., Wang, H.: Monoxide: scale out blockchains with asynchronous consensus zones (2019). https://www.usenix.org/conference/nsdi19/presentation/wang-jiaping

15. Xi, J., et al.: A blockchain dynamic sharding scheme based on hidden Markov model in collaborative IoT. IEEE Internet Things J. **10**(16), 14896–14907 (2023). https://doi.org/10.1109/JIOT.2023.3294234
16. Xie, C., Yan, L., Li, W., Zhang, Z.: Distributed power-law graph computing: theoretical and empirical analysis (2014). https://proceedings.neurips.cc/paper/2014/hash/67d16d00201083a2b118dd5128d-d6f59-Abstract.html
17. Xu, M., Feng, G., Ren, Y., Zhang, X.: On cloud storage optimization of blockchain with a clustering-based genetic algorithm. IEEE Internet Things J. **7**(9), 8547–8558 (2020). https://doi.org/10.1109/JIOT.2020.2993030
18. Yang, Z., Li, M., Yang, R., Yu, F.R., Zhang, Y.: Blockchain sharding strategy for collaborative computing internet of things combining dynamic clustering and deep reinforcement learning (2022). https://doi.org/10.1109/ICC45855.2022.9838570
19. Zamani, M., Movahedi, M., Raykova, M.: RapidChain: scaling blockchain via full sharding (2018). https://doi.org/10.1145/3243734.3243853
20. Zhang, C., Wei, F., Liu, Q., Tang, Z.G., Li, Z.: Graph edge partitioning via neighborhood heuristic (2017). https://doi.org/10.1145/3097983.3098033
21. Zhang, Z., et al.: A community detection-based blockchain sharding scheme (2022). https://doi.org/10.1007/978-3-031-23495-8_6

Distributed Photovoltaic Power Generation Prediction Based on Feature Extraction and Multi-model Fusion

Zhenjiang Pang[1], Zhaowu Zhan[1(✉)], Minglang Wu[1], Fei Jin[2], and Yuanyang Tang[1]

[1] China Gridcom Co., Ltd., Shenzhen 518000, China
zhanzhaowu@sgchip.sgcc.com.cn
[2] Shenzhen Smart-Chip Microelectronics Technology Company Ltd., Shenzhen 518048, China

Abstract. With the improvement of photovoltaic grid-connected power generation and the accelerated development of distributed photovoltaics, distributed photovoltaic power generation prediction plays an important role in guaranteeing the safety and stability of power grid operation. Accurate distributed photovoltaic power generation prediction is highly important, and distributed photovoltaic power generation is affected by the combination of several meteorological variables, so the deep feature extraction of meteorological variables is very critical. This paper proposes a meteorological feature extraction method for distributed photovoltaic power generation prediction and a photovoltaic power generation prediction model based on residual connection fusion of multiple models. The feature extraction method enriches the model's input by performing deep feature extraction on time, meteorological, and power generation data using statistical methods, feature cross, periodic information, approximate entropy, and photovoltaic panel temperature feature extraction methods. In the model construction, a multi-model fusion method based on residual connection is established. Firstly, a softmax regression prediction model based on KNN is proposed. Then, the overall structure of the model integrates similar day regression prediction models, TabNet, XGBoost, RandomForest, and LightGBM models, and through residual connection and multi-layer stacking, the accuracy of photovoltaic power generation prediction is continuously improved. Experimental results show that the feature extraction method and the model proposed in this paper are superior to other models, and can effectively improve the accuracy and stability of distributed photovoltaic power generation prediction.

Keywords: Distributed Photovoltaic Power · Feature Extraction · Skip Connect · Forecasting · Tabnet · Xgboost · Similar Day

1 Introduction

With the acceleration of China's low-carbon energy transformation and the advancement of energy system reform, new energy generation technologies have gradually become mainstream generation technologies, of which photovoltaic power generation is a very important part of new energy.

K. Ye and L.-J. Zhang (Eds.): ICIOT 2023, LNCS 14208, pp. 47–63, 2024.
https://doi.org/10.1007/978-3-031-51734-1_4

48   Z. Pang et al.

According to 2021 statistics, China's photovoltaic power generation grid-connected installed capacity reached 306 million kilowatts, ranking first in the world, of which the installed capacity of distributed photovoltaics has exceeded 100 million kilowatts, accounting for about one-third of the total photovoltaic power grid-connected installed capacity. It is expected that the installed capacity of distributed photovoltaics will exceed that of centralized photovoltaics in the future. Therefore, distributed photovoltaic power generation has become an important way of new energy power generation in China.

Photovoltaic power generation technology is complex and has many influencing factors, in which the power generation of distributed photovoltaics is affected by a variety of factors such as climate, meteorology, and geographical environment and other factors. The degree of influence of each factor is different in different environments. In terms of influencing factors, the power generation of distributed photovoltaics is not only affected by solar radiation intensity and temperature, but also by cloud cover, humidity, wind speed, pressure, and photovoltaic panel temperature. Moreover, the degree of influence of each influencing factor changes dynamically with meteorological conditions and time. It is precisely because the power generation of distributed photovoltaics is affected by various factors, the uncertainty of influencing factors as well as the strong randomness, which leads to the instability of distributed photovoltaic power generation. Accurate prediction of distributed photovoltaic power generation can effectively solve the instability of distributed photovoltaic power generation, and plays a vital role in the safe and stable operation of the power grid. It also plays an important role in the absorption of new energy, load regulation and so on.

With the development of meteorology and artificial intelligence, most scholars use machine learning and deep learning methods [3, 4] to forecast photovoltaic power generation, combined with numerical weather forecast (NWP). Currently, the focus is mainly on distributed photovoltaic power generation prediction, which can be divided into two categories from the perspective of modeling logic. One is the mechanism-driven method, which establishes a prediction model based on physical principles from meteorological information and photovoltaic system parameters [5]. The other is the data-driven method, which builds a prediction model by analyzing the relationship between historical output [6, 7], NWP information and other data [8–10]. Literature [11, 12] proposes a physical calculation model for distributed photovoltaic power generation, based on solar radiation, meteorological factors, and photovoltaic panel's own parameters. The output power is calculated through the physical model. However, most distributed photovoltaics lack photovoltaic panel's own parameters, which makes it impossible to use the model. At the same time, the physical model in the prediction problem completely depends on the weather forecast data, which is insensitive to weather changes, resulting in low prediction accuracy. Literature [13–17] uses general machine learning methods such as multivariate regression, SVM, and LightGBM, etc. However, machine learning methods cannot effectively learn the deep features of meteorological and historical power data, resulting in low final prediction accuracy. Literature [18–20] uses time-series deep learning methods, which cannot effectively learn the relationship between the influence of meteorological data and power generation, resulting in low prediction accuracy and poor stability. Literature [21, 22] proposes a prediction model based on weather types, but the prediction accuracy is relatively low, since it is difficult to classify the predicted date into a certain weather type in the prediction stage, especially for cloudy and rainy. Moreover, there is a certain degree of error in the forecasting data itself.

Therefore, the existing methods mainly have the following problems: Firstly, the complex and diverse influencing factors of distributed photovoltaic power generation make it difficult for general feature extraction methods to support stable and accurate power generation prediction. Secondly, in feature extraction, the lack of temporal features, the interaction between multiple variables, and periodic features hinders the accuracy of power generation prediction. Thirdly the physical model-based method for distributed photovoltaic power generation prediction requires real-time acquisition of physical quantities, which is difficult to implement in practice. Finally the data-driven method is often biased towards a certain aspect, which is not enough to solve the problem of distributed photovoltaic power generation prediction.

To address the above issues, this paper proposes a feature extraction method for distributed photovoltaic power prediction. The method includes approximate entropy-based fluctuation feature extraction of historical power series, time-based cycle feature construction and temperature-based photovoltaic panel temperature feature construction. These methods can effectively and comprehensively extract the deep features of meteorological data and historical power generation, and solve the problems of few features and insufficient model learning.

In addition, this paper proposes a softmax regression prediction model based on KNN and a multi-model fusion method based on residual connection. The method integrates similar day prediction models, TabNet, XGBoost, and RandomForest, etc. It adopts residual connection (skip-connect) and Stacking integration methods between layers to gradually improve the accuracy and stability of model prediction.

The rest of this paper is organized as follows. First, we provides a detailed description of the feature extraction method in Sect. 2. Afterward, Sect. 3 describes the proposed prediction method using residual connections and multi-model fusion. The single model and multi-model fusion methods are introduced separately. Finally, we evaluate and compares the proposed methods through experiments in Sect. 4 and then summarize the findings of the paper.

2   Feature Extraction

Feature extraction is a critical step in the construction of distributed photovoltaic power generation prediction models, directly impacting the convergence of model training and prediction accuracy. This paper proposes a set of feature extraction methods for distributed photovoltaic power generation prediction, including statistical, feature cross, periodic, and information entropy-based methods.

2.1   Multi-dimensional Information Extraction

A set of multi-dimensional features are constructed for the multivariate data of meteorological data and historical photovoltaic power generation, including statistical features of partial variables, feature cross features of multivariate variables, and trend features of multivariate variables.

Statistical Features: The meteorological factors or historical power generation affecting the power of distributed photovoltaic are time-series variables. Based on the historical sequence values of the variables, new statistical features are constructed using statistical methods, including maximum value, mean, kurtosis coefficients, and skewness coefficients. For example, the statistical features are calculated for the sequence $\{I_{t-m-1}, I_{t-m}, \ldots, I_{t-1}\}$ of the radiation intensity variable at time t, which is composed of the first m historical values of the radiation intensity variable.

Cross Features: There are many factors affecting distributed photovoltaic power generation, and these factors may interact with each other. Therefore, constructing cross features between different variables, forming combinations of different features, can help the model to learn the relationship between variables. The cross feature is calculated as follows:

$$c_t = x_1^t \times x_2^t \tag{1}$$

where, c_t is the cross feature of two variables x_1^t and x_2^t at time t.

Trend Features: In the prediction of power generation at a certain time point, the trend of the influencing factors is very important information, which will affect the change of power generation at the predicted time point. Therefore, constructing the trend features of variables can help the model learn effective information, improve the accuracy and generalization ability of the prediction model. The construction of trend features is as follows:

$$v_t = h\left(x_t^1, x_t^2\right) = \frac{x_t^1 - x_{t-w}^1}{x_t^2 - x_{t-w}^2 + c} \tag{2}$$

In the above equation, x_t^1 and x_t^2 are two variables at time t, x_{t-w}^1 and $x_{t-w}^2 2$ are the values of the two variables before $t - w$, v_t is the trend feature of the two variables at time t; c is a large constant, and the value in this paper is 50.

2.2 Periodic Feature

Distributed photovoltaic power generation is affected by meteorological conditions, so the changes in meteorological conditions and photovoltaic power generation have strong periodicity, and there is an obvious periodicity in time. This periodic information is an important feature information for the prediction model, so the time information is processed, including month, week, day, and hour. The time stamp of the power generation is extracted to obtain the month (m), week (w), day (d), and hour (h) of the year.

Use the sine and cosine trigonometric functions to construct periodic features based on month, week, day, and small period, then tranform the original discrete time features into periodic sequences, as shown in the following equation:

$$\begin{cases} z_{sin} = \sin\left(2\pi \times \frac{z}{z_{max}}\right) \\ z_{cos} = \cos\left(2\pi \times \frac{z}{z_{max}}\right) \end{cases} \tag{3}$$

where z is the input time feature (such as month, week, day, or hour); z_{max} is the maximum value of the corresponding time feature, with the maximum values for month, week, day, and hour being 12, 53, 366, and 24, respectively.

2.3 Extract Volatility Feature

In distributed photovoltaic power generation forecasting, from the perspective of time series, the future power generation has a certain relationship with the historical power generation, and the power generation at the time point before and after has a certain causal relationship [11]. Therefore, the historical power generation is an important feature information. After the historical power generation sequence is extracted, it can be input into the prediction model to improve the performance of the prediction model.

Entropy is used to measure the degree of chaos or randomness of a system. The smaller the entropy value is, the more certain the system is. The larger the entropy value is, the more chaotic the system is. Therefore, the historical power generation sequence can be used to extract information from the entropy, and this paper uses approximate entropy to extract sequence information. The feature calculation pseudocode is as follows:

Algorithm 1: Approximate entropy calculation

Input: A sequence $S_N \leftarrow \{s_1, s_2, ..., s_N\}$ of length N, distance threshold r_0, and subsequence length M

Output: AE

1:     **for** $m \leftarrow m$ to $m + 1$ **do**

2:         $z(i) \leftarrow \{s_i, s_{i+1}, s_{i+2}, ..., s_{i+m}\}$

3:         $Z_{N-m+1} \leftarrow \{z(1), ..., z(i), .., z(N-m+1)\}$

4:         $D_{(N-m+1)\times(N-m+1)} \leftarrow d_m\big(z(i), z(j)\big)$

5:         $C_i^m(r_0) \leftarrow \dfrac{num[d_m(z(i), z(j)) < r_0]}{N - m + 1}$

6:         $\Phi_m(r_0) \leftarrow \dfrac{\sum_{i=1}^{N-m+1} log(C_i^m(r_0))}{N-m+1}$

7:     **end for**

8:     $AE \leftarrow \Phi_{m=m}(r_0) - \Phi_{m=m+1}(r_0)$

The following steps can be used to extract approximate entropy features from historical sequences based on the above pseudocode:

Step 1: Set the length of the historical power generation sequence $S_N = \{s_1, s_2, \ldots, s_N\}$, and define the distance threshold r_0 and the subsequence length m.

Step 2: Reconstruct the original sequence S_N into $N - m + 1$ subsequences $\{z(1), z(2), \ldots, z(N - m + 1)\}$ of length m, where the subsequences are represented by $z(i)$, and $z(i) = \{s_i, s_{i+1}, s_{i+2}, \ldots, s_{i+m}\}$.

Step 3: Calculate the distance $d_m(z(i), z(j))$ between any two reconstructed subsequences $z(i)$ and $z(j)$ and obtain the distance matrix $D_{(N-m+1)\times(N-m+1)}$, where $1 \leq j \leq N - m + 1$, including the distance between $i = j$, where the distance calculation method can be customized, and in this paper, the maximum difference between corresponding elements in two sequences is used.

Step 4: Count the number of satisfying the following conditions and calculate the ratio between the total number of statistics:

$$C_i^m(r_0) = \frac{num[d_m(z(i),z(j)) < r_0]}{N-m+1} \tag{4}$$

Step 5: Calculate the average similarity rate for subsequences of length m:

$$\Phi_m(r_0) = \frac{\sum_{i=1}^{N-m+1} \log(C_i^m(r_0))}{N-m+1} \tag{5}$$

Step 6: Calculate the average similarity rate for subsequences of length $m+1$ based on steps 1–5 above: $\Phi_{m+1}(r_0)\Phi_{m+1}(r_0)$.

Step 7: The approximate entropy of the historical power generation sequence is: $AE = \Phi_m(r_0) - \Phi_{m+1}(r_0)$.

2.4 Photovoltaic Panel Temperature Characteristics

According to the photovoltaic power generation mechanism, factors affecting power generation are not only meteorological conditions, photovoltaic panel area, conversion rate, etc., but also the temperature of photovoltaic panels, which is an important factor affecting power generation. Therefore, this paper constructs the temperature of photovoltaic panels through physical models. The temperature T_{NWP} in the meteorological data set is used as an approximate substitute for the ambient temperature T_{amb}, then can obtain an estimate of the operating temperature T_C of photovoltaic panels [11]:

$$T_C = T_{amb} + \frac{I_t}{I_{NOCT}}(T_{C,NOCT} - T_{amb}) \tag{6}$$

where: $T_{C,NOCT}$ is the temperature of the photovoltaic panel under the nominal environment, which is generally taken as 20 °C. I_{NOCT} is the irradiance under the nominal environment, which is generally taken as 800 W/m². I_t is the irradiance at a certain time, which is replaced by the irradiance in the meteorological forecast.

3 Method

This paper proposes a power generation prediction method based on residual connection and multi-model fusion. The overall framework of the model is shown in Fig. 1. First, in the first layer (Layer1), a similar day distributed photovoltaic power generation regression prediction is performed based on the original dataset $D_{raw}\langle X, Y \rangle$. At the same time, the original dataset $D_{raw}\langle X, Y \rangle$ is extracted to obtain $D'\langle X', Y \rangle$. In the second layer (Layer2), the output of the similar day prediction and the dataset $D'\langle X', Y \rangle$ after feature extraction are used as input to construct multiple models of distributed photovoltaic power generation prediction models, and predict the output separately. Finally, in the third layer (Layer3), the output of the multi-models in the second layer and the original dataset $D\langle X, Y \rangle$ are used to construct the output layer LightGBM model. The final prediction result of the LightGBM model is used as the prediction value of distributed photovoltaic power generation.

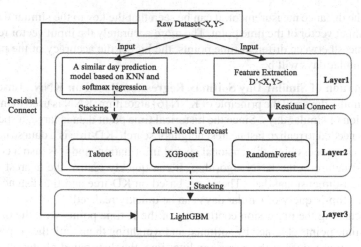

Fig. 1. The framework of the model

3.1 KNN-Softmax Prediction

Based on the theory of similar days and the principle of photovoltaic power generation, if the influencing factors of distributed photovoltaic power generation are the same, the power generation value is bound to be the same. For example, if two time points have the same temperature, irradiance, humidity, geographical environment, photovoltaic panel area, and season, the power generation values of the two time points must be very close. Therefore, in the prediction stage, the similar historical time points to the prediction time point can be found, and the power generation values of the historical similar time points can be used as the prediction values. In order to ensure the stability of the model, the attention idea is adopted to take the top-K similar time points, and then the prediction value is calculated by softmax. The model is expressed as follows:

$$y = f(q, K, V) = softmax\left(\frac{1}{d(q,K)_{Top-k}}\right) \times V \qquad (7)$$

where: q is the vector of the prediction time point; K and V are the vectors of the historical time points and the corresponding power generation values of the historical time points; d is the distance measurement method.

Distance Measurement. In this paper, L2 (Euclidean) distance is used for measurement. At the same time, L2 distance is sensitive to outliers, and makes similar points easier to distinguish in high-dimensional space.

$$d(X, Y) = \sqrt{\sum_{i=1}^{n}(x_i - y_i)^2} \qquad (8)$$

where: X and Y are the input vectors of a time point, respectively; x_i is the i-th element of vector X; y_i is the i-th element of vector Y.

From the distance measurement, it can be seen that the key to the similar day theory lies in the input vector of the time point. The more accurately the input vector represents the differences between different time points, the higher the accuracy of the prediction based on similar days will be.

Implementation of Similar Day Softmax Regression Based on KNN. Based on the theory of similar days and the principle of KNN [6] algorithm, KNN is used to implement the prediction of similar days. Since the historical time point data is large, a special data structure is needed to realize fast nearest neighbor search. KD-tree is a data structure that can efficiently process high-dimensional spatial information, and it is also a commonly used data structure in the KNN algorithm. It can quickly realize the nearest neighbor query of high-dimensional data. Therefore, based on KD-tree and the distance defined in 2.1.1, the Top-K query of similar days can be quickly realized.

By calculating the regression coefficients of the K time points with the distance of the Top-K time points obtained by softmax, and weighting them with the corresponding power generation values at the corresponding time, the distributed photovoltaic power generation prediction based on similar day regression can be realized.

3.2 Multi-model Fusion Based on Residual Connection

In order to improve the accuracy of the model, this section mainly adopts the idea of residual connection to fuse multiple models to realize the prediction of distributed photovoltaic power generation. Due to the differences between the principles of different models, although trained on the same dataset, the prediction results are different. If this difference is used well, it can not only improve the final prediction effect, but also improve the stability of the prediction, and the generalization ability of the model is stronger.

This paper uses three different models to predict distributed photovoltaic power generation, using RandomForest [7], XGBoost [9] and Tabnet [10], three models with relatively large differences.

3.3 Stacking-Based Fusion Prediction Model

Tabnet. Tabnet is a table data learning model based on attention mechanism. It not only has the advantages of deep learning, but also has the interpretability of traditional machine learning. Tabnet can realize feature engineering through FeatTranformer, avoiding manual feature engineering, effectively utilizing the advantages of deep learning to extract deep features. After feature extraction, the features are used in the decision step. Based on the attention mechanism, the most relevant features are found to realize instance-based important feature selection, and the most prominent features are learned. This makes the model have high performance on table data and also has interpretability.

The overall structure of Tabnet is shown in Fig. 2, where the encoder is composed of multiple FeatTransformers and multiple AttentiveTransformers stacked together. Figure 2(a) shows that the input to the encoder is processed numerical features, and the output consists of encoded features and data for final decision-making. Figure 2(b) shows that the Step in the decoder represents a decision step, similar to a decision node in a decision tree. Each Step receives all features of the input, and uses the output of the previous Step to weight the data features. The final output is used for final decision-making by accumulating the results of each Step.

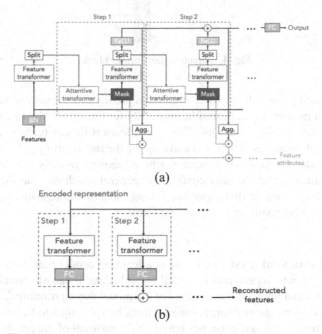

(a)

(b)

Fig. 2. The structure of the Tabnet ((a): Encoder, (b): Decoder)

The Feature Transformer in the Tabnet structure adopts two different modules: Shared across decision steps and Decision step dependent. The structure first uses Shared across decision steps for processing, and further uses Decision step dependent for processing, as shown in Fig. 3.

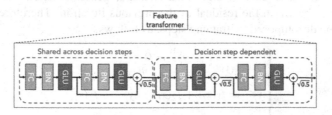

Fig. 3. Feature transformer block

The Attentive Transformer structure is used for feature selection, and outputs sparse importance representations of each feature through a fully connected layer, normalization layer, and Sparsemax, as shown in Fig. 4.

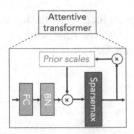

Fig. 4. Attentive transformer block

For distributed photovoltaic power generation prediction, Tabnet can learn the deep features of each meteorological variable, especially for the case with large data volume, the effect is better. At the same time, Tabnet can learn different features according to the differences of instances, which can make up for the shortcomings of manual feature extraction, the shortcomings of general machine learning models that are not based on instance learning, and the shortcomings of general machine learning models for underlearning large data. In this paper, the Tabnet model is represented by T, which is the Tabnet prediction result, in the following form.

$$Y_T = T(X) \tag{9}$$

XGBoost and RandomForest. XGBoost is a learning model based on the boosting ensemble strategy, which performs very well on table data. It can effectively reduce the bias of the model and improve the accuracy of the model during training. The main idea of XGBoost is to generate multiple regression trees by splitting and training features in the data. Each tree learns and generates based on the residual of the previous round. Its model definition is as follows:

$$\hat{y}_i = \sum_{k=1}^{K} f_k(x_i), f_k \in F \tag{10}$$

where: x_i is the i-th sample, f_k is the k-th tree model, K is the total number of trees, and F is the function space of all regression trees.

Since XGBoost is an additive model, each iteration generates a new tree model. The next iteration is based on the residual of the previous iteration. Therefore, the above Eq. (10) can be decomposed by training steps, as follows:

$$\begin{cases} \hat{y}_i^{(0)} = 0 \\ \hat{y}_i^{(1)} = f_1(x_i) = \hat{y}_i^{(0)} + f_1(x_i) \\ \hat{y}_i^{(2)} = f_1(x_i) + f_2(x_i) = \hat{y}_i^{(1)} + f_2(x_i) \\ \vdots \\ \hat{y}_i^{(t)} = \sum_{k=1}^{t} f_k(x_i) = \hat{y}_i^{(t-1)} + f_t(x_i) \end{cases} \tag{11}$$

Equation (11) is the iterative form of XGBoost in the training process, where: $\hat{y}_i^{(t)}$ is the prediction value in the t-th round, which is equal to the prediction value in the previous t-1 rounds plus the prediction result of the current round $f_t(x_i)$. $f_t(x_i)$ is the t-th tree, which is the regression tree to be generated in the t-th iteration.

The objective function of XGBoost consists of main two parts, namely the loss function part and the regularization part. The loss function part mainly makes the model fit better, while the regularization part is to punish the complexity of each tree, making the model simpler, preventing overfitting, and making its generalization performance better. The objective function is as follows:

$$Obj^{(t)} = \sum_{i=1}^{n} l\left(y_i, \hat{y}_i^{(t)}\right) + \sum_{k=1}^{t} \Omega(f_k) \tag{12}$$

In this Eq. (12), $l\left(y_i, \hat{y}_i^{(t)}\right)$ is the loss function part, which can be customized, but requires that the second-order derivative can be calculated; $\Omega(f_k)$ is the regularization part, which controls the complexity of each tree. The specific form is as follows:

$$\Omega(f_k) = \gamma T + \lambda \frac{1}{2} \sum_{j=1}^{T} w_j^2 \tag{13}$$

where, T is the number of leaf nodes, γ is the penalty coefficient, λ is the regularization penalty coefficient, and $\frac{1}{2} \sum_{j=1}^{T} w_j^2$ is the L2 regularization of leaf node scores.

Random Forest is a learning model based on the Bagging ensemble strategy. It is an effective way to reduce the model variance during training. It learns different decision functions in multiple random subspaces, reducing the model bias while improving the model's generalization ability. Its pseudocode is as follows:

Algorithm 2: The Construction of RandomForest Regression

Input: Dataset D, number of submodels K

Output: K integrated tree models $\{T_k\}_{k=1}^{K}$

1:     **for $k \leftarrow 1$ to K do**
2:         Sample D with replacement to obtain D^*
3:         Generate T_k through CART tree based on D^*
4:     **end for**
5:     Regression prediction: $y \leftarrow \frac{1}{K}\sum_{k=1}^{K} T_k(x)$

XGBoost and Random Forest have significant differences in ensemble strategy and training process. It can be considered that they focus on reducing bias and variance, respectively. Therefore, the fusion of the two can improve the prediction accuracy while enhancing the generalization ability of the prediction.

In distributed photovoltaic power generation forecasting, XGBoost model can effectively improve the accuracy of predictions, while Random Forest can improve the stability of predictions while ensuring accuracy. At the same time, for smaller datasets, XGBoost and Random Forest also perform well, which makes up for the shortcomings of Tabnet's poor results on small datasets. In this paper, G is used to represent XGBoost and R to represent Random Forest, in the following form:

$$Y_G = G(X) \tag{14}$$

$$Y_R = R(X) \tag{15}$$

Stacking-Based Fusion Prediction Model. The methods of distributed power generation prediction based on similar days and distributed photovoltaic power generation prediction based on multiple models have their own advantages and solve corresponding problems. Therefore, it is very necessary to effectively fuse them to achieve higher-precision distributed photovoltaic power generation prediction.

The method of distributed power generation prediction based on similar days can well correct the missing values and abnormal values of the target variable, especially when there are many missing values, the processing of missing values or abnormal values is not reasonable, and it can carry out a better secondary correction treatment to initially predict the distributed photovoltaic power generation. Based on the distributed photovoltaic power generation prediction based on similar days and feature engineering, the multi-model distributed photovoltaic power generation prediction can learn the hidden information after feature engineering, further improve the prediction accuracy. Finally, the predictions of multiple models are fused, and the original input is used to further fine-tune the predictions of multiple models, to achieve higher-precision distributed photovoltaic prediction.

This paper adopts the Stacking ensemble strategy and residual connection to fuse three-layer models, and the overall model framework is shown in Fig. 1. First, the first layer performs load prediction $Y_S = S(X)$ on the original input data on similar day (where S is the similar day prediction model, Y_S is the prediction result of the similar day on the original input) and feature extraction:

$$X' = F(X) \tag{16}$$

where F represents the feature extraction process, X' is the output after feature extraction, and the original input X is extended with features.

In the second layer, the prediction results and feature extraction results of the first layer are merged as the input of the second layer, and are respectively input to Tabnet, XGBoost and Random Forest models, then the prediction results Y_T, Y_G and Y_R are output respectively:

$$\begin{aligned} X_{L2} &= Concat(X', Y_S) \\ Y_T &= T(X_{L2}) \\ Y_G &= G(X_{L2}) \\ Y_R &= R(X_{L2}) \end{aligned} \tag{17}$$

In the third layer, the prediction values of the second layer are merged and further input to the LightGBM model in combination with the original input, and the final prediction result is output:

$$\begin{aligned} X_{L3} &= Concat(X, Y_T, Y_G, Y_R) \\ Y' &= LightGBM\,(X_{L3}) \end{aligned} \tag{18}$$

4   Experiments

This experiment uses one and a half years of distributed photovoltaic user data from a certain power company, including numerical weather forecast (NWP) data and historical power generation curve data from each distributed photovoltaic user. The data sets are all at a time resolution of 1 h. The data set is divided into a training set (April 21, 2021 to May 31, 2022) and a test set (June 1, 2022 to June 20, 2022), and feature extraction, model training, testing, and effect comparison analysis are carried out.

4.1   Evaluation Indicators

This paper mainly uses five indicators, including mean square error (MSE), root mean square error (RMSE), mean absolute error (MAE), mean absolute percentage error (SMAPE) and goodness of fit (R2), to comprehensively evaluate the model error. The calculation methods are as follows:

$$e_{MAE} = \frac{1}{n} \sum_{i=1}^{n} |y_i - \hat{y}_i| \tag{19}$$

$$e_{MSE} = \frac{1}{n} \sum_{i=1}^{n} (y_i - \hat{y}_i)^2 \tag{20}$$

$$e_{RMSE} = \sqrt{\frac{1}{n} \sum_{i=1}^{n} (y_i - \hat{y}_i)^2} \tag{21}$$

$$e_{SMAPE} = \frac{100\%}{n} \sum_{i=1}^{n} \frac{|y_i - \hat{y}_i|}{\frac{|y_i| + |\hat{y}_i|}{2}} \tag{22}$$

$$R^2 = 1 - \frac{\sum_i (y_i - \hat{y}_i)^2}{\sum_i (\bar{y}_i - y_i)^2} \tag{23}$$

where y_i is the true value of sample i, $\hat{y}_i$ is the predicted value of sample i, and $\bar{y}_i$ is the mean value of the sample set. Among them, the smaller the values of e_{MAE}, e_{MSE}, e_{RMSE} and e_{SMAPE}, the better the prediction performance of the model. The closer the R^2 value is to 1, the better the prediction performance of the model.

4.2   Impact Analysis of Feature Extraction

The original input meteorological data and historical power curve data are extracted to generate a new feature variable dataset. RandomForest, XGBoost, and TabNet are used to compare the performance before and after feature extraction. The evaluation indicators are adopted in Sect. 3.1, as shown in Table 1. It can be analyzed that after feature extraction, RandomForest, XGBoost, and TabNet all perform better than before feature extraction in all evaluation indicators. The SMAPE indicator can be improved by 0.03, 0.04, and 0.05, respectively. Therefore, the feature extraction method proposed in this paper is very effective and significantly improves the accuracy of the model prediction.

Table 1. Comparison results of feature extraction and model effects

Metric	Raw Data				Featured Data			
	RandomForest	XGBoost	TabNet	**Proposed**	RandomForest	XGBoost	TabNet	**Proposed**
MAE	0.1563	0.1688	0.1781	**0.1544**	0.1154	0.1071	0.1685	**0.0953**
MSE	0.0839	0.0998	0.0911	**0.0818**	0.0410	0.0361	0.0896	**0.0311**
RMSE	0.2896	0.3159	0.3018	**0.2860**	0.1832	0.1901	0.2993	**0.1763**
SMAPE	0.1112	0.1191	0.1574	**0.1056**	0.0836	0.0799	0.1019	**0.0688**
R^2	0.8670	0.8418	0.8556	**0.8703**	0.9324	0.9427	0.8779	**0.9507**

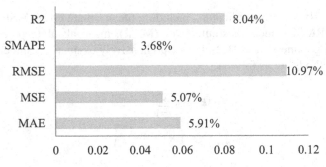

Fig. 5. The model improves in metrics

4.3 Performance Analysis

The performance of RandomForest, XGBoost, TabNet, and the proposed method is compared using the evaluation indicators in Sect. 3.1. The prediction performance is compared based on the original dataset (before feature extraction) and the dataset after feature extraction, as shown in Table 1. It can be analyzed that in the performance on the original dataset, all indicators of our proposed model are better than other models, and the performance of our proposed model is also significantly better than other models on the dataset after feature extraction. At the same time, the indicators of our proposed model have also been significantly improved before and after feature extraction, as shown in Fig. 5. MAE is reduced by about 0.059, MSE is reduced by about 0.05, RMSE is reduced by 0.11, SMAPE is reduced by 0.0368, and R2 is increased by about 0.08. Therefore, the multi-layer model fusion power generation prediction model proposed by this paper can effectively improve the accuracy of distributed photovoltaic power generation, and it also has good stability.

Comparison of the prediction results of the multi-layer model fusion power generation prediction model proposed by this paper before and after feature extraction. It also extracts the first 5 days of prediction results from the test set for visualization, as shown in Fig. 6 and Fig. 7. It can be clearly seen that the predicted power curves of our proposed model after feature extraction are closer to the real power generation curves on 2022-06-03 and 2022-06-04. When there are fluctuations in power generation, our proposed multi-layer model fusion power generation prediction model has better prediction performance, stability, and accuracy.

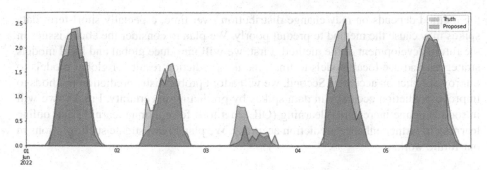

Fig. 6. Predict results based on the original dataset

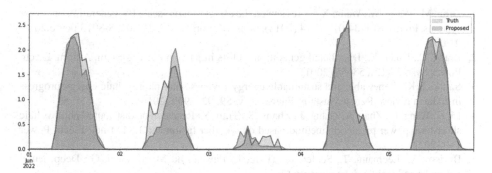

Fig. 7. Prediction results based on feature extraction

5   Conclusion and Future Directions

This paper proposes a variety of feature extraction methods for distributed photovoltaic power generation prediction. These methods include:

- Basic feature construction based on multi-dimensional information.
- Fluctuating feature extraction based on the historical output sequence of approximate entropy.
- Periodic features construction based on time.
- Photovoltaic panel temperature features construction based on temperature.

This paper also proposes a power generation prediction model based on residual connection and multi-model fusion. This model combines a similar day prediction model based on KNN and softmax regression and multiple models with different differences, such as Tabnet, XGBoost, and RandomForest. Finally, this paper conducts an experimental analysis based on the actual distributed photovoltaic power generation data from a certain region of a power company.

The proposed method solved the main problem of low prediction accuracy for distributed photovoltaic power generation, assuming that power generation will not change significantly over time, the main focus is on the model's ability to predict offline data. However, in real-world applications, the weather data and power generation data that the method depends on may change distribution over time, especially short-term data spikes may cause the method to predict poorly. We plan to consider the above issues in the future development of the method. First, we will introduce global and local models strategies, and use local models to fine-tune the prediction results of global models to improve prediction accuracy. Second, we will adopt probabilistic prediction methods to improve prediction accuracy in data spikes by predicting uncertainty. Finally, we will introduce online incremental learning (OIL) methods for continue learning and online learning to further enhance prediction accuracy. We plan to investigate such solutions in our future work.

References

1. Ding, M., Wang, W., Wang, X.: A review on the effect of large-scale PV generation on power systems. Proc. CSEE **34**(01), 1–14 (2014). https://doi.org/10.13334/j.0258-8013.pcsee.2014.01.001
2. Liang, C., Duan, X.: Distributed generation and its impact on power system. Autom. Electr. Power Syst. **25**(12), 53–56 (2001)
3. Sahoo, S.K.: Renewable and sustainable energy reviews solar photovoltaic energy progress in India: a review. Renew. Sustain. Energy Rev. **59**, 927–939 (2016)
4. Li, F., Wang, L., Zhao, J., Zhang, J., Zhang, S., Tian, Y.: Research on distributed photovoltaic short-term power prediction method based on weather fusion and LSTM-net. Electr. Power 1–9 (2022)
5. Borisov, V., Leemann, T., Seßler, K., Haug, J., Pawelczyk, M., Kasneci, G.: Deep neural networks and tabular data: a survey (2021)
6. Taunk, K., De, S., Verma, S., Swetapadma, A.: A brief review of nearest neighbor algorithm for learning and classification. In: 2019 International Conference on Intelligent Computing and Control Systems (ICCS), pp. 1255–1260 (2019). https://doi.org/10.1109/ICCS45141.2019.9065747
7. Ali, J., Khan, R., Ahmad, N., Maqsood, I.: Random forests and decision trees. Int. J. Comput. Sci. Issues (IJCSI) **9** (2012)
8. Liu, X., Wang, J., Yao, T., Chi, X., Wang, X., Li, K.: A Distributed photovoltaic power prediction system based on time series data processing. Front. Data Comput. **3**(04), 140–148 (2021)
9. Chen, T., Guestrin, C.: XGBoost: a scalable tree boosting system. In: Proceedings of the 22nd ACM SIGKDD International Conference on Knowledge Discovery and Data Mining (KDD 2016), pp. 785–794. Association for Computing Machinery, New York (2016)
10. Arik, S.Ö., Pfister, T.: TabNet: attentive Interpretable tabular learning. In: AAAI 2021, vol. 35, pp. 6679–6687 (2021)
11. Wang, B., Lyu, Y., Chen, Z., Zhao, Q., Zhang, Z., Tian, J.: Automation of electric power systems. **46**(11), 67–74 (2022)
12. Zhao, B., Xue, M., Ge, X., Xu, W.: Research on calculating methods of output power of the photovoltaic system. Power Syst. Clean Energy **26**(07), 19–24 (2010)
13. Li, G., Liu, Z., He, J., Zhao, H., Zhang, S.: Study on the generator forecasting of grid-connected PV power system based on multivariate linear regression model. Mod. Electr. Power **28**(02), 43–48 (2011)
14. Fu, M., Ma, H., Mao, J.: Short-term photovoltaic power forecasting based on similar days and least square support vector machine. Power Syst. Prot. Control **40**(16), 65–69 (2012)
15. Mao, M., Gong, W., Chang, L., Cao, Y., Xu, H.: Short-term photovoltaic generation forecasting based on EEMD-SVM combined method. Proc. CSEE **33**(34), 17–24+5 (2013)

16. Liu, X., Wang, J., Yao, T., Zhang, P., Chi, X.: Ultra short-term distributed photovoltaic power prediction based on satellite remote sensing. Trans. China Electrotechnical Soc. **37**(07), 180 (2022)
17. Si, Z., Yang, M., Yu, Y., Ding, T., Li, M.: A hybrid photovoltaic power prediction model based on multi-source data fusion and deep learning. In: 2020 IEEE 3rd Student Conference on Electrical Machines and Systems (SCEMS), pp. 608–613 (2020)
18. Van Deventer, W., et al.: Short-term PV power forecasting using hybrid GASVM technique. Renew. Energy **140**, 367–379 (2019)
19. Niccolai, A., Dolara, A., Ogliari, E.: Hybrid PV power forecasting methods: a comparison of different approaches. Energies **14**, 451 (2021)
20. Abdel-Nasser, M., Mahmoud, K.: Accurate photovoltaic power forecasting models using deep LSTM-RNN. Neural Comput. Appl. **31**(7), 2727–2740 (2017). https://doi.org/10.1007/s00521-017-3225-z
21. Ye, L., Pei, M., Lu, P., Zhao, J., He, B.: Combination forecasting method of short-term photovoltaic power based on weather classification. Autom. Electr. Power Syst. **45**(01), 44–54 (2021)
22. Dai, Q., Duan, S., Cai, T., Chen, C., Chen, Z., Qiu, C.: Short-term PV generation system forecasting model without irradiation based on weather type clustering. Proc. CSEE **31**(34), 28–35 (2011)

A Pioneering Approach to Data Integration at Shanghai Exchange Group

Youwei Zheng[✉] and Min Ji

Shanghai Exchange Group, Shanghai 200062, China
zhengyouwei@suaee.com

Abstract. In the dawn of the digital era, society has unanimously acknowledged data as an enterprise's central asset. Shanghai Exchange Group has crafted an innovative data management framework upon its existing infrastructure. This framework seamlessly intertwines File Space, Graph Space, and Vector Space, bridging the gap between heterogeneous data structure domains. Not only does it provide a potent and precise pathway for extracting value from unstructured data, but also intuitively it unveils the embedded semantic relationships within the data. With this progressive upgrade, the pioneering infrastructure is set to revitalize Shanghai OneNet Trade. This strategic initiative will establish a solid foundation for forthcoming innovations, enriching customer engagements while simultaneously enhancing our competitive edge in the digital trading sphere.

Keyword: data management · data platform · dataops workflow · retrieval-augmented generation

1 Background and Strategic Significance

In the face of accelerating digital transformation, global cities and businesses are formulating strategies to enhance their core competitive strengths. On September 8, 2023, Shanghai Municipal People's Government officially unveiled the establishment of Shanghai Exchange Group, signaling a steadfast commitment to enhancing the allocation of economic resources and advancing data-driven innovation [1].

The inception of Shanghai Exchange Group transcends the mere adoption of digitization; it embodies a major paradigm shift and progressive evolution in the management of public resource exchange. A pivotal element of this transformation is the development of a unified data platform, integral to the initiative for trading and regulatory platforms [2].

Both Shanghai Municipal People's Government and Shanghai Exchange Group acknowledge that conventional data platforms and management systems fall short in meeting the complex transactional demands of today's digital landscape. Therefore, the strategic importance of a cutting-edge data platform is greatly amplified, which is anticipated to elevate the internal management mechanisms of Shanghai Exchange Group and exert a transformative influence on Shanghai's public resource exchange ecosystem, setting new benchmarks for efficiency, transparency, and innovation.

K. Ye and L.-J. Zhang (Eds.): ICIOT 2023, LNCS 14208, pp. 64–71, 2024.
https://doi.org/10.1007/978-3-031-51734-1_5

2 Innovative Approach to Data Integration

2.1 Embrace RAG

Traditional data platforms have served as the foundational pillar, catering to the basic data requirements of enterprises. These mature technologies, predominantly tailored for structured data or tabular tables, have provided enterprises with robust storage and retrieval capabilities. However, the onset of the digital era has ushered in a paradigm shift, resulting in an array of diverse data categories and formats, particularly with a significant surge in text data. This expansion is not just quantitative but also extends to the depth and complexity of the data. Consider the equity trading facilitated by the Shanghai United Assets and Equity Exchange as an example. Behind these texts, there is also crucial information such as the emotions of the recipients, the historical context of the project's implementation, and the perspectives of supervisory bodies. These textual datasets serve as rich reservoirs of crucial insights, which capture the emotions of the involved parties, the historical backdrop of project implementation, and the viewpoints of overseeing bodies. To unlock the value within this intricate tapestry of text, it is imperative to embrace a more cohesive approach, underpinned by advanced frameworks and methodologies. The challenge lies not just in handling the sheer volume of data, but in deciphering the similarties embedded within, to discover the full potential of the information at our disposal.

The Retrieval-Augmented Generation (RAG) serves as the pinnacle of progress in the information retrieval and natural language processing, marking a groundbreaking shift in these overlapping disciplines [3]. By integrating Information Retrieval (IR) with Large Language Models (LLMs), RAG surpasses the capabilities of traditional keyword-based search and regular matching techniques, offering more relevant and precise results. LLMs, as innovative forerunners in the realm of modern natural language processing, boast an exceptional ability to understand and generate human-like language. This development paves the way for opportunities in interactions that are both user-centric and intuitive. Nevertheless, LLMs face challenges, particularly a shortfall in specialized, enterprise-specific knowledge when tackling domain-specific subjects or industry-specific terminology. Thus, the integration of LLMs with IR becomes crucial. This synergy enables LLMs to access, engage with, and extract insights from both structured and unstructured corporate data repositories, effectively bridging the existing knowledge gap [4].

RAG employs vector databases to thrive in the sphere of data retrieval and management, especially in the face of mounting data volumes and intricacies. Vector databases convert data into vector format and utilize similarity scores for query processing, which significantly enhances query speed, as well as semantic accuracy and relevance. This effectively addresses the limitations of traditional bag-of-words retrieval methods [5]. For instance, traditional relational databases often struggle with complex queries involving multiple fuzzy parameters, sometimes even stumbling over simple queries. Currently, the traditional search on the official website of Shanghai Exchange Group is inadequate for meeting customer needs. As illustrated in Fig. 1, it only supports title-based searches, and at times, fails to return even the most basic matches. Conversely, RAG facilitates a multi-faceted output, offering users a higher degree of similarity in target results, thereby enhancing satisfaction among those in pursuit of historical project data retrieval.

Vector databases distinguish themselves by rapidly aligning query data, thereby fortifying RAG technology's capacity to probe user queries more profoundly and furnish contextually pertinent information. This collaboration effectively bridges user requirements with the existing data landscape. Although not without limitations, chief among them being the potential for partial results mainly due to reliance on similarity metrics, vector databases offer a blend of speed and accuracy that renders them invaluable in modern data management and business intelligence. As we navigate an ever-evolving amalgamation of data challenges, RAG technology crystallizes as a revolutionary answer, steering organizations towards adaptability and efficiency in better managing their data assets. Despite its constraints, RAG currently serves as the sole avenue for interaction with LLMs, making it an essential adoption for databases poised to confront the digital era's intricate challenges.

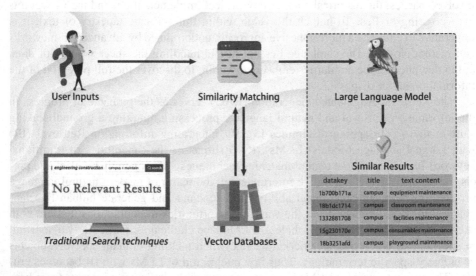

Fig. 1. Technical framework and practical application of Retrieval-Augmented Generation

2.2 Integrated Structural and Non-Structural Management

In light of the rising complexity of data and the growing necessity to support RAG, we have acknowledged the pressing need for a holistic management approach for both structured and unstructured data. Drawing upon advanced paradigms and meticulous research, we have conceived and implemented an innovative enhancement based on the existing DataOps framework, aiming for a resilient and sustainable data delivery [6]. The paramount feature of this enhanced version lies in its strategic utilization of file objects as the primary representatives for unstructured data, ensuring a flawless integration with the structured data abstraction systems. This enhancement introduces "File Space" paradigm, a sophisticated architecture designed to register individual file objects while linking data columns of those objects to their respective file spaces. This innovation allows for the effortless access and dissemination of unstructured data resources across a myriad of table columns, facilitated by the simple activation of the corresponding file space within the DataOps workbench. Beyond mere data sharing, this groundbreaking development amplifies the overall efficiency and agility of data management.

However, the integration of structured and unstructured data goes beyond simple confines of storage and management. As depicted in Fig. 2, our approach integrates file object IDs as structured scalars directly into DataOps workflow. Such integration ensures a smooth melding of unstructured data with its structured counterparts during streamlining, processing and the entire dataflow. It fosters a closer alignment with established practices of structured data governance and minimizes the learning curve for users. To bolster the processing for unstructured data, we have engineered a suite of commonly utilized processing components for unstructured data. These tools offer a spectrum of functionalities, ranging from annotative labeling to content extraction. They facilitate the automatic extraction of critical information from a diverse array of office document formats, such as Excel, Word and PDF, while in parallel intelligently generating tags and keywords based on the content. Leveraging the capabilities of vector databases, we have introduced "Vector Space" into the workbench, achieving a harmonious integration and synergy with the database. This integration has paved the way for full-text indexing capabilities within the workbench, significantly elevating the speed and accuracy of unstructured data retrieval. The feature ushers in a new era of operational efficiency in our data management systems.

By meticulously implementing the aforementioned technical strategies, we have achieved a comprehensive enhancement in the integrated management of structured and unstructured data. This ensures a highly efficient data management process, spanning from data storage to application layer. Moreover, our innovative framework addresses not only management requirements of unstructured data, but also achieves integrated management of its metadata. This precise orchestration and integration of metadata guarantees the integrity, accuracy, and real-time nature of the managed data. In this intricate process, RAG technology plays an indispensable role. It acts as a robust channel, facilitating the interaction between structured & unstructured data. Thanks to RAG, we are empowered to extract, retrieve, and interpret key information from unstructured data in real time. This extracted information can then be smoothly combined with the metadata of structured data. Significantly, our framework paves the way for an innovative synthesis of structured data and metadata from unstructured data, culminating in the creation of a so-called meta-knowledge system. This unified system enhances the fluidity and efficiency of data processing and its subsequent operations. It enables us not just to extract invaluable information from the data but also to delve deeper, understanding the profound knowledge and logic underpinning the data at the metadata level.

2.3 Enhanced Master Data Management with Graph Data

Through our comprehensive engagement in the field of enterprise data management, we've acquired deep-seated expertise in orchestrating both structured and unstructured data landscapes. Additionally, we've recognized the pivotal role that RAG technology

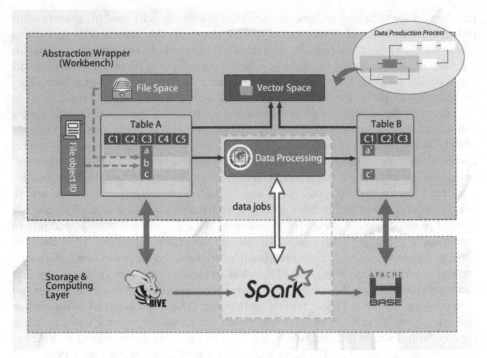

Fig. 2. Integrated framework for structured and unstructured data governance

plays in enhancing data services and elevating business applications to new levels of complexity and capability. Building upon this solid foundation, we are advancing our data platform through strategic refinements in master data management (MDM), specifically by integrating and aligning it with cutting-edge graph data technology. MDM is a crucial component in contemporary enterprise architecture. Master data serves as both "authoritative source" and "unified view", forming the bedrock of enterprise data ecosystem. Accurate and reliable master data is imperative, ensuring that all business units operate based on a consistent and unified data version [7]. However, the evolving landscape of data complexity is outpacing the capabilities of traditional MDM methods, rendering them inadequate for the demands of enterprises. It is especially evident when using relational databases to house master data. In such scenarios, the intricate relationships between data points often escape capture and expression. This issue parallels the challenges which are outlined above regarding the management and utilization of unstructured data. Our journey into advanced data management practices highlights the need for innovative approaches to uphold the integrity and utility of master data in an increasingly complex data environment.

Graph database has emerged as a pivotal solution to elevate the efficacy of master data management. Unlike traditional relational databases, graph technologies have the distinctive way of articulating the relationships between entities, offering a more intuitive and efficient portrayal of data connections. Building on our approach with unstructured data, we've devised an integration strategy to weave graph data into the DataOps framework for streamlined data jobs management, as depicted in Fig. 3. This weave eliminates the necessity for auxiliary data synchrony or transformation workflows. Thus, the graph database isn't just an isolated storage module but evolves into a central component of the workbench. This harmonious integration facilitates its symbiotic existence alongside structured and unstructured data repositories.

From a technical vantage point, our innovative framework is enriched with bespoke components designed for both 'node data' and 'edge data.' These components autonomously discern and harvest relational elements, subsequently transmuting them into their corresponding graph counterparts in accordance with predefined parameters. This automated transformation process not only diminishes the reliance on manual setups but also assures swift and precise data transposition. Moreover, drawing parallels to the file space, we've unveiled the "Graph Space" conceptual architecture to bolster the management capabilities of our graph database. Each graph space represents a distinct graph database instance. To aid this, the workbench introduces a Graph Space Editor, granting users the ability to architect, initiate, and oversee graph spaces in a visually engaging milieu, thereby offering a more tactile grasp on master data management.

When assessing graph technology alongside alternatives such as vector databases, the advantages and limitations of each come into sharper focus. While vector databases demonstrate a robust capability for managing high-dimensional data and executing

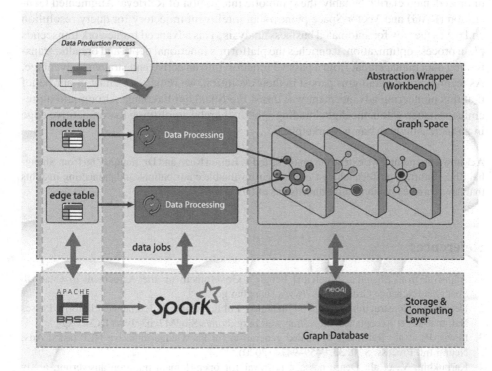

Fig. 3. Integrated fusion of graph spaces in the DataOps framework

specific mathematical operations, they tend to falter in articulating and probing the labyrinthine relationships among data entities. In contrast, graph database excels in the intuitive rendering and nuanced navigation of complex data connections. RAG technology, critical to both data analytics and business operations, harmonizes seamlessly with graph database architecture, revealing unprecedented depth of insight into data associations. This synergetic fusion not only strengthens the bedrock of data management but also ensures organizations possess the advanced tools needed for thorough data exploration and effective asset utilization, thereby paving the way for more enlightened and strategic decision-making.

3 Discussion

In an epoch increasingly defined by digital transformation, data has metamorphosed from a mere informational byproduct to a keystone of agility and digital ingenuity. Navigating the intricate terrain of structured, unstructured, and graph data presents a formidable quandary: how to cohesively manage, meld, and extract their latent value. Our research and practice dive deep into Shanghai Exchange Group's avant-garde data management architecture, an integrated framework which encompasses File Space, Graph Space and Vector Space across an integrated platform. This harmonious fusion doesn't merely elevate the governance of unstructured data; it illuminates complex data interrelations with unprecedented clarity. Notably, the symbiotic integration of Retrieval Augmented Generation (RAG) and Vector Space pioneers an intelligent trajectory for query resolution and paves the way for automated business analysis. This advanced framework transcends plain process optimization; it enriches the platform's functional depth and breadth, transmuting data management from a passive function into an active and strategic advantage. As technological paradigms persist in their evolution, we remain steadfast in our belief that this pioneering advancement will thrust the Shanghai Exchange Group into a preeminent stance within the digital trading sphere, thereby amplifying its competitive edge in an increasingly dynamic marketplace.

Acknowledgement. We extend our gratitude to Dr. Beijun Ruan and Dr. Jianqiu Zhu from Shanghai Zhizi Information Technology Co. For their invaluable contributions and pioneering insights that have enriched the innovative dimensions of this work.

References

1. Approval from Shanghai Municipal People's Government on the Agreement to establish Shanghai Exchange Group. https://www.shanghai.gov.cn
2. Deepening Construction Project of Shanghai Public Resource Exchange Platform Passes National-Level Acceptance. https://mp.weixin.qq.com/s/Sjo3M7vn3cJyAYDC-4xAgg
3. Lewis, P., et al.: Retrieval-augmented generation for knowledge-intensive NLP tasks. Adv. Neural Inf. Process. Syst. **33**, 9459–9474 (2020)
4. Karpukhin, V., et al.: Dense passage retrieval for open-domain question answering. arXiv preprint arXiv:2004.04906 (2020)

5. SparckJones, K.: A statistical interpretation of term specificity and its application in retrieval. J. Doc. **28**(1), 11–21 (1972). https://doi.org/10.1108/eb026526
6. Zheng, Y.: Digital transformation drives high-quality development of shanghai OneNet trade. China High Tech **21**, 103–106 (2022)
7. Loshin, D.: Master data management. Morgan Kaufmann, Burlington (2010)

DigitalPlantMan: A Multi Process Manufacturing Task Management System for Digital Plant

Hongyu Tian[1,2] , Yuan Wang[3], and Kejiang Ye[1(✉)]

[1] Shenzhen Institute of Advanced Technology, Chinese Academy of Sciences,
Shenzhen 518055, China
kj.ye@siat.ac.cn
[2] University of Chinese Academy of Sciences, Beijing 100049, China
[3] College of Mathematics and Information Science, Hebei University,
Baoding 071002, China

Abstract. In recent years, with the rapid development of the new generation of information technology and the acceleration of economic globalization, all industries and enterprises are facing the urgent need of digital transformation. The implementation of a digital plant production management system has become a major boost to industry transformation and development. Leveraging contemporary computer technology and integrating it with traditional manufacturing processes can enhance process intelligence and management efficiency. In pursuit of implementing such a system, our research has designed and developed a multi process manufacturing task management system - DigitalPlantMan for digital plant, utilizing cutting-edge software development frameworks like Spring Boot and Vue. This paper presents the step-by-step system development process which includes an analysis of system requirements, functional design, database design, and implementation of each system module. Finally, testing results indicate that the system facilitates efficient business collaboration on a unified platform, thereby assisting enterprises in enhancing their digital and intelligent manufacturing capabilities to achieve safety, greenness, efficiency, and flexibility.

Keywords: Industrial Internet · Digital Manufacturing · Factory Task Management · Spring Boot · Vue

1 Introduction

Currently, global industrial production is under rapid transformation. The evolution of information technology, particularly Digital Twin (DT) technology, is increasingly bridging the gap between traditional industrial production and contemporary digital systems [17]. The rapid development of the new generation of information technology has brought new opportunities to the fields of traditional industry and manufacturing [9]. Digital plant production is gradually becoming an important direction for optimizing and upgrading factory production. With the support of information technology, factory production management has developed a new management model, which combines information management platforms with traditional factory production. The implementation of the digital plant production management system has become an important boost for industry transformation and development, relying on the application of computer technology [19].

In real-world industrial contexts, numerous factories necessitate substantial manpower and resources for operation. This often leads to ambiguous production and sales processes, inadequate control over production procedures, and excessive manual intervention on production lines. Additionally, issues such as unreasonable production plan arrangements can be encountered. These factors contribute to low management efficiency within the factory and ineffective management of relevant information regarding the factory's production tasks. From a management perspective, a production management system can allow managers to manage factory production information more intuitively and conveniently, monitor production dynamics, make decisions and adjustments in a timely manner based on data feedback, and improve efficiency [6]. From a production perspective, a production management system can standardize production management and business process optimization, improve the efficiency of factory production task management, reduce production errors, and achieve the goal of building an efficient, energy-saving, and comprehensively managed digital plant [8].

To solve a series of problems in many manufacturing factories, such as increasing production and management costs, complex production process management, and difficulty in coordinating between factory production and client demands, we design and implement a multi process manufacturing task management system - DigitalPlantMan for digital plant. DigitalPlantMan allows clients to order the products they need through this system and view the production progress of orders in the system. Employees can allocate production tasks to the factory based on client orders and record the progress of production processes through this system. Administrators can manage personnel information and machine information. Through the implementation of these functions, factories can transition from traditional manual production mode to modern digital production mode, improve the efficiency of enterprise production and operation activities, improve the efficiency of factory production management, reduce employee burden, reduce production labor costs, and make business communication between clients and factories more concise and convenient.

The reminder of this paper is organized as follows: In Sect. 2, we present related work in the area of Industrial Internet. The methodology of system development is shown in Sect. 3. The design of the system is introduced in Sect. 4. In Sect. 5, we describe the implementation of each module of the system. In Sect. 6, we test the functionality and compatibility of the system. Finally the conclusions are given in Sect. 7.

2   Related Work

Factory Digital Transformation. In [2], Henrik Blichfeldt et al. built a conceptual framework that links the adoption of digital technology, the innovation of product and service, and competitive advantage, with a focus on the process industries. The findings suggest that higher levels of digital technology implementation lead to more radical product and service innovations, particularly in low-tech sectors, ultimately improving performance and competitive advantage. In terms of factory digital transformation, Medema et al. [12] explore the challenges and considerations related to the transition from analog to digital control systems in nuclear power plants, with a focus on human reliability analysis (HRA), and the need to adapt HRA methods to address unique opportunities for human error associated with digital control technologies, as well as emerging vulnerabilities of cyber threats.

Manufacturing IT. The digital transformation of the manufacturing industry has derived the concept of manufacturing IT. Li et al. [7] point out that manufacturing IT includes the algorithms and softwares that are used by the production system and also the hardware infrastructure such as sensors and actuators that provide intelligent monitoring and control over physical machines. It also includes production management systems that incorporate different technologies and manage all the data generated throughout the manufacturing process. The authors in [4] propose a digital twin enhanced industrial Internet (DT-II) reference framework for smart manufacturing and discuss the implementation and operation mechanism from three perspectives, including the product lifecycle level, the intra-enterprise level and the inter-enterprise level.

Applications of Digital Transformation in Manufacturing Industry. Liu et al. [10] introduce a new collaborative data management framework that enables digital twin for metal additive manufacturing systems. The framework facilitates supports intelligent process monitoring, control, and optimization, reduces development times and costs, and improves product quality and production efficiency. Pashentsev et al. [15] develop innovative mechanisms for environmental monitoring in industrial enterprises, utilizing mathematical methods and modern digital smart systems, aiming to address environmental challenges and improve the overall quality and efficiency of manufacturing activities. In [18], the authors implement a Cloud-Edge-End System (CEESys), which not only facilitates remote real-time monitoring of industrial environments but also provides effective management through remote control. Liu et al. [11] present YOLO-IMF, an enhanced version of the YOLOv8 algorithm, tailored for surface defect detection on aluminum plates. This method outperforms both YOLOv5m and Faster R-CNN in recognizing surface defects.

While the aforementioned research has made significant contributions to the digital transformation of industries across various levels, a notable gap exists in the management of process tasks within factories. The multi process manufacturing task management system introduced in this study offers a comprehensive approach to managing digital factories.

3 Methodology

3.1 Development Process

The multi process manufacturing task management system is a front-end and back-end separation project. The development process of this project is mainly as follows:

- **a. Requirements analysis**
  Consulting relevant literature, collecting data, analyzing system requirements, and designing system functions.
- **b. Functional design**
  Based on system research and requirement analysis, design the system's functions, determine the specific content of each business function in the system, gradually achieve the expected functions, and complete the system architecture.
- **c. System design**
  The primary objectives of system design encompass the creation of a system framework structure, designing the system database, developing the system functions, and designing the user interface for the system.
- **d. Coding and implementation of the system**
  Develop software programs to execute the functions of each module, ensuring they meet the requirements for functionality, performance, interface, and other facets of the target system.
- **e. Software testing**
  Conduct functional testing in accordance with the initial requirements, and conduct a thorough analysis of any issues that may arise. Additionally, perform compatibility testing.

3.2 Primary Technologies

Spring Boot. Spring Boot is a new development framework based on Spring provided by the Pivotal team, which further encapsulates Spring. Its main purpose is to simplify the initial construction and development process of Spring applications, making the development, testing, and deployment of applications easier [21]. Spring Boot is the starting point for all Spring based development projects. The main feature of Spring Boot is that it follows the principle of "agreed upon due to configuration". With minimal or default configuration required, it is possible to use embedded Tomcat [3] and Jetty [13] servers without the need to deploy war files. It provides customized initiator Staters, simplifies Maven configuration, and provides production level service monitoring solutions such as security monitoring, application monitoring, health detection, etc.

Vue. As a front-end framework technology, is a progressive framework used to build user interfaces. One of Vue's main characteristics is that it follows the MVVM pattern. MVVM is a data-driven view and a bidirectional data binding principle [1]. MVVM, an acronym for Model, View, and ViewModel, is a methodology that partitions each HTML page into three distinct sections: the model layer, the view layer, and the view model layer. The primary function of the model layer is to extract and process returned data, while the view layer predominantly manages page display. In between these two layers, the view model layer serves as a bridge. It responds to user events by dispatching requests to the model layer for data acquisition. Concurrently, it transforms the data retuned by the model layer into the visual representation seen on the page [14].

MySQL Database. The system's back-end data storage is facilitated through the use of MySQL 5.7, a relational database management system [5] that opts for storing data across various tables rather than a single, expansive warehouse. This approach enhances both speed and flexibility. The SQL language, which is predominantly utilized for accessing databases, is also integral to MySQL's functionality. Owing to its compact size, rapid performance, minimal overall cost of ownership, and notably open-source nature, MySQL software is frequently selected as the website database for the development of small to large-scale websites.

Browser/Server Structure. In Browser/Server structure, the logic and data of the application program are stored on the server, so the browser only needs to make a request to the server. The web server responds to the request, operates on the database, and returns the data to the browser. After obtaining the web page, the web page is displayed in the browser [16]. The main characteristics of Browser/Server architecture are high dispersion, simple development, high sharing, easy maintenance, and low total cost of ownership.

3.3   Development Approach

The back-end of DigitalPlantMan is predominantly developed using the Spring Boot framework, bolstered by scenario-specific dependencies integrated during application inception. This approach streamlines the configuration process, as Spring Boot automatically configures the application based on these dependencies. Consequently, the development of an autonomous Spring application is expedited, eliminating the need for extensive manual configuration.

On the front-end, Vue is adopted as the development framework, chosen for its lightweight nature that facilitates a simplified learning curve. Vue seamlessly amalgamates HTML, CSS, and JS into cohesive components, promoting their efficient reuse across various parts of the system. This integration significantly enhances the overall development process by fostering component and page-level reusability.

MySQL is employed as the system's database management solution, offering an open-source alternative without incurring additional costs. Leveraging optimized SQL query algorithms, MySQL enhances query and data processing speeds, rendering it well-suited for diverse information management functions within the system. This technological choice affirms the system's feasibility and aligns with best practices in software development. The complete software framework is shown in the Fig. 1.

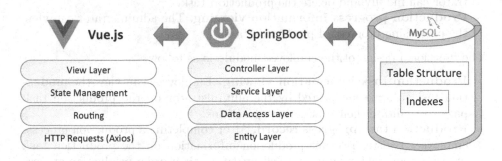

Fig. 1. Software framework

4 System Design

4.1 Design of System Function

DigitalPlantMan is primarily segmented into three components: the client, employee, and administrator modules. The client module allows clients to access information regarding factory production products, issue orders, and monitor the progress of their orders through the system. Conversely, employees can initiate production tasks and track their progress via the employee module. The administrator module enables administrators to handle personnel data, add, delete, or modify details pertaining to employees and clients. Additionally, they have the authority to oversee product information and production machinery details, document factory-produced product information, and convert customer orders into production tasks which can then be published. The functional design of the administrator module is as follows:

- **Personnel management.** The administrator manages personnel information within the system on the personnel management page, including adding new user information, deleting and modifying existing personnel information in the system.
- **Product management.** The administrator has the capability to add product-related information or to modify and delete existing product details. The data added is subsequently displayed on the product information module page.

- **Machine information management.** The administrator can add and modify machine information.
- **Order information viewing.** The administrator is granted access to view information pertaining to client orders.
- **Production task arrangement.** After receiving a client order, the administrator publishes the production task on the production task page based on the content of client order. After the administrator arranges the production order, the client order status is displayed as in processing, and the administrator can modify and delete the production task.
- **Production progress information viewing.** The administrator can view the processing progress of production tasks.

The functional design of the employee module is as follows:

- **Production task information viewing.** Employees can view the production task information posted by the administrator on the production task page to facilitate their production operations.
- **Production task progress record.** After completing a production process, employees register relevant production information on the production task progress page, making it easy for clients to see their order production process and for administrators to manage production information.

The functional design of the client module is as follows:

- **Order release.** The client initiates the order through the system's order release interface. Using the existing product information, the client submits the necessary product orders. Once an order begins production, it becomes non-modifiable and cannot be deleted. If clients have specific requirements, they can provide notes on the task orders.
- **Order progress viewing.** The client can view the content of the order and the completion time on the production task progress page.

4.2   Design of System Database

Conceptual Design of Database. The database management system used in DigitalPlantMan can be divided based on the functional modules of the system. In this article we use E-R diagrams for data structure analysis, also known as entity relationship diagrams, which provide a method to represent entity types, attributes, and relationships, used to describe the conceptual model of the real world [20]. The E-R diagrams of the system user module, machine module, order module, product module, production task module, and production task item module are shown in Fig. 2.

Logical Design of Database. After the conceptual structure design of the database is completed, we transform the conceptual structure into the actual data model supported by a certain database system, which is the logical structure of the database [22]. The database relation schemas are shown in Table 1, Table 2, Table 3, Table 4, Table 5 and Table 6, respectively.

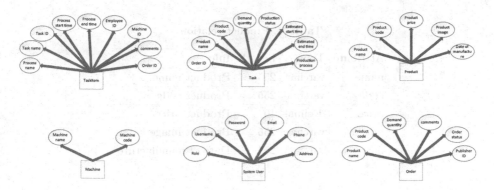

Fig. 2. E-R diagrams

Table 1. System user relation

Attribute	Type	Length	Info
username	varchar	50	Username
password	varchar	50	Password
email	varchar	50	Email address
phone	varchar	50	Phone number
address	varchar	255	Address
role	varchar	50	Role

Table 2. Machine relation

Attribute	Type	Length	Info
name	varchar	255	Machine name
code	varchar	255	Machine ID

Table 3. Order relation

Attribute	Type	Length	Info
name	varchar	255	Product name
code	varchar	255	Product code
num	int	11	Demand quantity
comments	varchar	255	Comments
status	varchar	255	Order status
userid	int	11	Publisher ID

Table 4. Product relation

Attribute	Type	Length	Info
name	varchar	255	Product name
code	varchar	255	Product code
price	decimal	10	Product price
img	varchar	255	Product image
date	varchar	255	Date of manufacture

Table 5. Task relation

Attribute	Type	Length	Info
name	varchar	255	Product name
code	varchar	255	Product code
num	int	11	Demand quantity
status	varchar	255	Production status
start	varchar	255	Estimated start time
end	varchar	255	Estimated end time
content	varchar	255	Production process
ordersid	int	11	Order's ID

Table 6. Task item relation

Attribute	Type	Length	Info
name	varchar	255	Process name
taskname	varchar	255	Task name
taskid	int	11	Task ID
start	varchar	255	Process start time
end	varchar	255	Process end time
userid	int	11	Employee ID
machineid	int	11	Machine ID
comments	varchar	255	comments
ordersid	int	11	Order's ID

5 System Implementation

The system's implementation is segmented into three distinct components: the client module, employee module, and administrator module. The client module allows users to access product information, release orders, and monitor the progress of order production. The employee module enables employees to initiate production tasks and track their progress within the system. Meanwhile, the administrator module is tailored for managing personnel data, enabling administrators to add or remove employee and client details, as well as modify product information and production machine details. Additionally, they can record product information and convert clients' orders into production tasks, which are then published within the system. The login page of the system is shown in Fig. 3.

5.1 Implementation of Administrator Module

Administrators can manage all personnel information in the system, as shown in Fig. 4. Upon clicking the "Add" button situated in the upper-left corner, a user information addition pop-up box will appear. This box requires the input of relevant details based on varying identities. Once filled, the user is displayed on the administrator's personnel information management page. The administrator has the ability to modify and delete personnel data by utilizing the "Edit" and "Delete" buttons located on the right side of the personnel information box. Upon clicking the "Edit" button, an editing box will be presented to the system. In contrast, clicking the "Delete" button prompts a pop-up box for confirmation of deletion. Administrators have access to add, modify, delete, and verify product-related information regarding machines, orders, tasks, and the factory's production process. To add new product data to the system, click the "Add"

Fig. 3. Login page

button. This action will also trigger a pop-up box. For modifications and deletions of product data, use the "Edit" and "Delete" buttons located on the right side of the product information box.

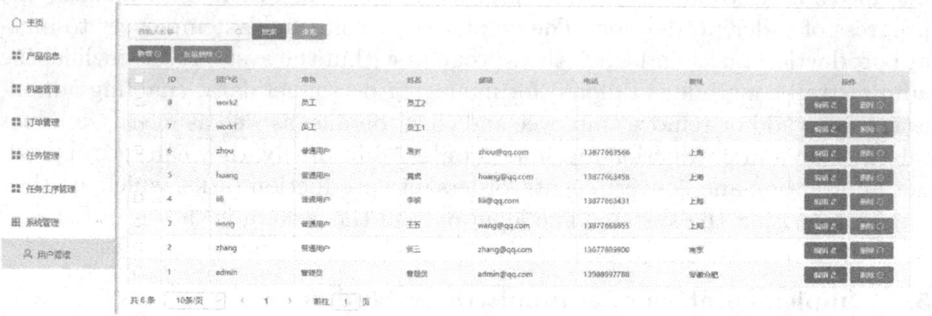

Fig. 4. Administrator module

5.2 Implementation of Employee Module

Figure 5 shows the system management interface for the employee module. The left-hand navigation bar encompasses various functions of the employee backend system, primarily including the employee homepage, production task management page, and production task process record page. Distinct buttons lead to different functional interfaces, yet the overall layout remains constant. The "Production Task Management" page displays tasks issued by the administrator. Employees can modify the production status according to the current production circumstances. A status of "not started" signifies an unactivated production task. On clicking the "Production" button, the task status transitions to "Processing", indicating that the task is in progress. If the task status is "Processing", selecting the "Complete" button changes it to "Processing Completed", signifying that the task has been processed. Employees can document the completion status of different processes within a production task based on actual production circumstances. The process record automatically registers the number of employees involved in operations, with each employee registration recording a different number of workers. Task process records can be amended or deleted as necessary. Once an employee documents the process, it becomes visible in both the administrator module and client module, facilitating ease for administrators in managing production task progress and clients in verifying production progress information of their orders at any given time.

Fig. 5. Employee module

5.3   Implementation of Client Module

Figure 6 shows the client's system management interface. The navigation bar situated on the left-hand side of the screen serves various functions within the employee post system. These include access to the client homepage, product information viewing page, and order management page. Clients can utilize this page to peruse the product information that the factory offers for production. The administrator also has the ability to search for product information via a designated search box, allowing clients to place orders based on this information. Upon clicking on order management, clients have the option to publish their desired orders onto the system's database. It is important to note that the status of an order will change according to its processing status. If the order status is "unprocessed", clients are free to modify or delete it. However, if the order status is "in processing", clients cannot alter or delete the order. Instead, they can simply click on the "View" button to see the details of the order's processing status.

Fig. 6. Client module

6   System Testing

The primary objective of system testing is to ascertain whether the system's operation aligns with its functional requirements. Additionally, it aims to identify any undiscovered bugs within the system, thereby ensuring its quality. This process helps prevent operational issues once the system is released and can also help reduce maintenance costs.

6.1   Functional Testing

Functional testing, also referred to as black box testing, involves the comparison of software against a container whose contents remain unseen. This method allows for testing based solely on external displays, disregarding the internal structure of the software. Initially, test case design is conducted, followed by point testing according to the use case table to ensure the system functions in a normal manner.

Administrator Module Testing. Firstly, we evaluated the login function on the login page. Upon entering the administrator's account and password and clicking the "login" button, we successfully accessed the management page. Subsequently, we conducted a test on product information management. Upon arriving at the product information page, we clicked the "add" button, input the relevant test data, and then confirmed it by clicking the "confirm" button. The newly added product information subsequently appeared on the product information interface. If the product name was not provided, the product information could not be added. The name input box was highlighted in red, prompting the user to enter the product name. Lastly, we tested the production task management function. When clients published order information on the order management page, we clicked the "publish" button and input the corresponding production task data. After confirming it with another button, we accessed the production task management page to view the new production task information.

Employee Module Testing. Following the initial login test, we implemented a function to add and modify production task processes via the task process management page. Upon clicking the "add" button and inputting the relevant order details, the new order information is displayed on the task process management page. To successfully modify the production task process content, users should click the "edit" button, input the necessary changes in the pop-up window, and then confirm their modifications.

Client Module Testing. Initially, on the login page, clients can authenticate themselves using their unique username and password. Subsequently, we conducted a test to add orders on the client's order management page. By clicking the "Publish Requirements" button, they can enter the corresponding order information and then confirm by clicking the "Confirm" button. This will cause the new order information to appear on the order management page. The final test involved allowing the client to check the execution status of an order. Upon entering the order management page, they can click the "View" button located under the "Processing Details" section. At this point, a pop-up window will display the processing details of the order, providing them with detailed information regarding the order's status.

6.2 Compatibility Testing

The primary purpose of compatibility testing is to ascertain whether the system operates unimpededly across various browsers and whether it encounters any errors or loading failures. This system has been rigorously tested on both Chrome and 360 browsers, with tests conducted by adjusting the browser proportions. The results indicate that the system functions optimally without any issues such as code instability, layout discrepancies, crashes, or flashbacks.

7 Conclusion

In recent years, the swift advancement of next-generation information technology and the acceleration of economic globalization have necessitated digital transformation across various industries and enterprises. Digital plant production management systems have emerged as a pivotal element in this corporate digital evolution. Consequently, for effective system design, it is essential to tailor functions to the specific context while ensuring that the interrelation of each function is logical and apt. Leveraging software development technologies and integrating them with enterprise manufacturing processes can enhance operational intelligence, elevate management efficiency, and further elevate the digital prowess of the enterprise.

In this paper, we have designed and developed a multi process manufacturing task management system - DigitalPlantMan for digital plant. This system amalgamates personnel information management, production order management, production task arrangement management, and production schedule management. The aim is to enable factories to manage production data more intelligently, thereby enhancing production efficiency. Users can employ DigitalPlantMan to manage the factory's production and processing tasks in an intelligent manner. This not only simplifies online ordering and order tracking requirements for clients but also caters to the needs of factory staff for intelligent production and management. In future work, we plan to further refine existing modules and integrate them with a data analysis module for production and orders, aiming to create a more intelligent digital plant.

Acknowledgment. This work is supported by the National Key R&D Program of China (No. 2021YFB3300200), National Natural Science Foundation of China (No. 92267105), Guangdong Special Support Plan (No. 2021TQ06X990), Shenzhen Basic Research Program (No. JCYJ20200109115418592, JCYJ20220818101610023).

References

1. Anderson, C.: The Model-View-ViewModel (MVVM) design pattern. In: Anderson, C. (ed.) Pro Business Applications with Silverlight 5, pp. 461–499. Springer, Heidelberg (2012). https://doi.org/10.1007/978-1-4302-3501-9_13
2. Blichfeldt, H., Faullant, R.: Performance effects of digital technology adoption and product & service innovation-a process-industry perspective. Technovation **105**, 102275 (2021)
3. Brittain, J., Darwin, I.F.: Tomcat: The Definitive Guide: The Definitive Guide. O'Reilly Media, Inc. (2007)
4. Cheng, J., Zhang, H., Tao, F., Juang, C.F.: DT-II: digital twin enhanced industrial internet reference framework towards smart manufacturing. Robot. Comput.-Integr. Manuf. **62**, 101881 (2020)
5. DuBois, P.: MySQL. Addison-Wesley (2013)
6. Han, X., Liu, Y., Zhang, X., Cui, S.: Application of equipment intelligent management system in the construction of intelligent factories in the chemical industry. Chem. Enterp. Manag. 114–116 (2022)
7. Li, J.Q., Yu, F.R., Deng, G., Luo, C., Ming, Z., Yan, Q.: Industrial internet: a survey on the enabling technologies, applications, and challenges. IEEE Commun. Surv. Tutor. **19**(3), 1504–1526 (2017)
8. Li, J.: Feasibility analysis of student management information system. Electron. Technol. Softw. Eng. **03**, 237–242 (2023)
9. Li, Q., Tang, Q., Chen, Y., et al.: Research on the architecture, reference model, and standardization framework of intelligent manufacturing system. Comput. Integr. Manuf. (31), 539–549 (2018)
10. Liu, C., Le Roux, L., Körner, C., Tabaste, O., Lacan, F., Bigot, S.: Digital twin-enabled collaborative data management for metal additive manufacturing systems. J. Manuf. Syst. **62**, 857–874 (2022)
11. Liu, Z., Ye, K.: YOLO-IMF: an improved YOLOv8 algorithm for surface defect detection in industrial manufacturing field. In: He, S., Lai, J., Zhang, L.J. (eds.) METAVERSE 2023. LNCS, vol. 14210, pp. 15–28. Springer, Cham (2023). https://doi.org/10.1007/978-3-031-44754-9_2
12. Medema, H., Savchenko, K., Boring, R., Ulrich, T., Park, J.: Human reliability considerations for the transition from analog to digital control technology in nuclear power plants. In: 11th Nuclear Plant Instrumentation, Control, and Human-Machine Interface Technologies, NPIC and HMIT 2019, pp. 132–141 (2019)
13. Moshovos, A., Memik, G., Falsafi, B., Choudhary, A.: Jetty: filtering snoops for reduced energy consumption in SMP servers. In: Proceedings HPCA Seventh International Symposium on High-Performance Computer Architecture, pp. 85–96. IEEE (2001)
14. Ning, J.: Design of university task management system based on cloud platform and Vue. Electron. Technol. Softw. Eng. **14**, 247–250 (2022)
15. Pashentsev, D.A., et al.: Digital software of industrial enterprise environmental monitoring. Ekoloji Dergisi (107) (2019)
16. Shan, X.: Design and implementation of a multimedia communication system for web users. Master's thesis, Beijing University of Posts and Telecommunications (2019)
17. Tang, L., Ye, K.: DT-EEC: a digital twin-assisted end-edge-cloud collaboration architecture for industrial internet. In: 2022 IEEE Smartworld, Ubiquitous Intelligence & Computing, Scalable Computing & Communications, Digital

Twin, Privacy Computing, Metaverse, Autonomous & Trusted Vehicles (Smart-World/UIC/ScalCom/DigitalTwin/PriComp/Meta), pp. 1638–1643. IEEE (2022)

18. Tian, H., Ye, K.: CEESys: a cloud-edge-end system for data acquisition, transmission and processing based on HiSilicon and OpenHarmony. In: He, S., Lai, J., Zhang, L.J. (eds.) METAVERSE 2023. LNCS, vol. 14210, pp. 3–14. Springer, Cham (2023). https://doi.org/10.1007/978-3-031-44754-9_1

19. Wang, L.: Research on the improvement of gulf company's factory operation management system for intelligent manufacturing. Master's thesis, Yanshan University (2022)

20. Wang, Z., Li, P., Bao, Y., Li, J., Zhang, R.: Analysis and design of a tobacco sales queuing system. Comput. Knowl. Technol. **11**(16), 84–87 (2015)

21. Webb, P., et al.: Spring boot reference guide. Part IV. Spring Boot features **24** (2013)

22. Zhang, Y.: Design of the database for the enrollment management system of sports majors in universities. Inf. Technol. **06**, 42–45 (2014)

Multi-agent DSS for Smart Government Crisis Management

Hui Jiang(✉) ⓘ and Ying Wang

Shandong Technology and Business University, Yantai, Shandong Province, China
Jianghui0927@sdtbu.edu.cn

Abstract. The conventional government fails to acknowledge the paramount importance of data in crisis management. The Decision Support System (DSS) for intelligent governance can furnish decision makers with effective crisis decision support. The process of government crisis decision-making entails the pre-decision monitoring of big data on crisis information, situation simulation during the decision-making process, and post-decision evaluation and analysis, thereby establishing a cyclical framework. Building upon the conventional four-database structure, the multi-agent intelligent government crisis decision support system incorporates an additional case database. The Multi-Agent DSS system, comprising Interface Agent, Crisis Information Monitoring Agent, Crisis Incident Response Agent, Situation Simulation Agent, Decision-making Agent, Decision Evaluation Agent, Case Analysis Agent and Collaboration Agent, collaborates synergistically with the aid of data warehouse and artificial intelligence technology. The intelligent multi-agent decision support system (DSS) will significantly enhance the level of crisis management decision-making in traditional government settings, thereby improving the system's self-learning capabilities and effectively addressing vulnerabilities associated with crisis decision-making.

Keywords: Multi-Agent · Smart Government · Crisis Management · Crisis · Decision Support System

1 Introduction

In recent years, there has been a surge in public emergencies and catastrophic accidents that pose threats to public security worldwide. The unprecedented challenges brought by the novel coronavirus epidemic have put the crisis decision-making ability of government departments to an ultimate test. Consequently, crisis management has emerged as an urgent concern for governments globally. Crisis, also known as "emergency events" and "emergencies," refers to situations that pose a threat to national security, social life, people's interests, and specific circumstances related to them. In his book Policymaking in Adversity, the renowned policy scientist Yehel Droll once stated [1], "Crisis response (crisis decision-making) holds significant practical importance for many countries and potentially vital importance for all countries. The more widespread or deadly the crisis is, the more crucial an effective crisis response becomes. The decisions made during a crisis are highly important and mostly irreversible".

K. Ye and L.-J. Zhang (Eds.): ICIOT 2023, LNCS 14208, pp. 88–100, 2024.
https://doi.org/10.1007/978-3-031-51734-1_7

Government crisis decision-making entails the process through which governmental organizations, operating within constraints such as limited temporal, informational, and resource-related capacities, strive to exert control over the propagation of a crisis. This necessitates the integration of available resources, expeditious comprehension and analysis of public crisis events, and prompt implementation of specific measures to effectively address the crisis [2]. Compared to routine decision-making, government crisis decision-making is a distinctive form of decision-making that poses challenges in predicting its actual impact and entails significant risks. Government crisis decision support systems are particularly demanding due to the complexity of information involved and time constraints [3]. Enhancing the quality of government crisis decisions has emerged as a prominent topic in academic research.

2 Literature Review

2.1 Government Crisis Management

Since the 9/11 attacks in the United States in 2001, the importance of government crisis management has received widespread attention from scholars both domestically and internationally. Developed countries, led by the United States, have always emphasized a combination of theory and practice in their research on government crisis management. These researches can be divided into studies on crisis information and decision support, studies on crisis communication and utilization, studies on the construction of crisis information systems, as well as studies on the qualities and education of crisis management personnel [2].

Domestic scholars' research on government crisis decision support systems mainly focuses on the fields of computer science, information management, and public administration.

Scholars in the field of computer science primarily investigate the technical aspects of decision support systems, focusing on their architecture and system construction. They have conducted extensive research on the impact of new media on government decision-making, specifically exploring network communication, online supervision, and digital democracy. Furthermore, they have explored various perspectives including data warehousing, knowledge management, and sentiment analysis mining to develop government decision support systems [4]. As a result of their efforts, an online platform for monitoring public opinion in governmental affairs has been successfully developed [5].

Scholars in the field of information management have predominantly focused on studying decision support problems from the perspectives of management science and information technology. They have conducted research on government information resource management issues based on governmental decisions [6], developed knowledge management systems with a focus on decision-making for consulting agencies [7], and created government public decision support information systems [8]. Some scholars have applied Shannon's model from information theory to analyze the characteristics of information flow in government crisis decision-making, proposed a quantifiable model for such flow, and subsequently analyzed various aspects related to government crisis decision-making. Based on modern principles of crisis management, they have constructed an ideal model for a government crisis decision support system [3].

Scholars in the field of public management have extensively reviewed and evaluated research on government crisis management, conducting comprehensive and profound studies on issues such as the causes of government decision failures, the models and mechanisms that should be adopted for government decisions, etc. They have identified weaknesses in the information monitoring, warning, and collection capabilities of government crisis decision-making mechanisms. The optimal state for public crisis data backup is to achieve collaboration among multiple stakeholders [2]. It has been observed that during its initial exploration stage, China's government established a "crisis information disclosure-centered" model; however, it has yet to clarify the fundamental goal of public crisis information management - supporting government crisis decision-making [9]. Some scholars have proposed integrating the 'Emergency Management Case Library' into China's government emergency decision-making system, thereby constructing a 'two-case three-system' model for emergency decision-making based on both emergency plans and case libraries [10]. This entails enhancing decision-making procedures, establishing think tank institutions, implementing responsibility mechanisms for decision implementation, and fostering a robust service-oriented government decision-making mechanism to ensure seamless integration of decision-making authority and accountability [11].

After critically examining the aforementioned research literature, it becomes evident that the majority of scholars have approached the issue of government crisis decision support solely from their respective disciplinary backgrounds and limited research perspectives. This approach lacks a comprehensive understanding and appreciation of the distinctive nature of government crisis decision-making, as well as interdisciplinary integration, thereby impeding effective problem resolution in this process.

2.2 Decision Support System

The research and application of Decision Support Systems (DSS) have always been dynamic, with constant emergence of new concepts and systems. In recent years, the study and application of Artificial Intelligence (AI) technology has paved the way for novel avenues in knowledge learning and acquisition. For instance, Collaborative Case-Based Reasoning (CCBR) employed in multi-attribute decision-making methods enables cross-organizational utilization of case libraries, facilitating knowledge and resource sharing among diverse organizations to enhance the quality of knowledge acquisition and decision-making [12].

In a library of dispersed and massive cases, the attributes of cases are diverse and varied. CCBR can effectively address management issues such as establishing mechanisms for sharing case resources across multiple organizations, facilitating collaboration among multiple agents and systems, as well as optimizing collaboration among different levels and entities [13]. In the context of continuous advancements in big data and artificial intelligence technologies, the integration of data and knowledge to drive intelligentization and automation of information analysis methods has emerged as a pivotal research direction [14].

Under the guidance of Mr. Qian Xuesen, scholars have established an emergency intelligence integration seminar hall to foster a collaborative and integrated working environment for intelligence professionals [15]. Drawing on the principles of three-dimensional world theory and aiming to enhance decision-making in practical application scenarios, a sophisticated problem processing system was developed to address existing challenges in intelligent government intelligence decision-making. A case analysis was conducted to illustrate the implementation of an intelligent government intelligence decision-making system [16].

2.3 Smart Government and Intelligent Decision-Making

The process of government digital transformation, encompassing the integration of ICT in business operations, service delivery, and citizen engagement, entails a comprehensive and systematic overhaul of governance principles, methodologies, processes, tools, etc., as the government proactively adapts to the digital era. By fostering data sharing for promoting collaborative partnerships among businesses, its objective is to augment the modernization of governmental governance systems and capabilities. Some scholars also regard it as the utilization of information and communication technology by the public sector to enhance information dissemination and service provision, foster citizen engagement in decision-making processes, and facilitate a more accountable, transparent, and efficient governance [17]. From the perspective of service effectiveness, smart government services exhibit characteristics of intelligence and precision. During the stage of demand identification, government departments leverage artificial intelligence and big data technology to enhance efficiency and accuracy in identifying needs. In the stage of precise supply, there is a realization of meticulous coordination between departments and demands, facilitating the provision of accurate services. Government services are transitioning from previous extensive management towards targeted governance aimed at specific individuals and particular issues [18].

Drawing on field research conducted by domestic scholars, employing an embedded approach, this study examines the prevailing challenges in various stages of government data collection, sharing, utilization, openness, and services in China with a specific focus on Shanghai as a case study. Additionally, it investigates the technical, capacity-related, and institutional factors that contribute to these challenges. Consequently, this research further enhances the framework for effective governance of government data [19].

Furthermore, several studies have focused on developing integrated and comprehensive intelligent service systems based on implementation strategies. For instance, in the domain of emergency disaster reduction research, they have successfully implemented services such as emergency rapid adaptive mapping, typical disaster knowledge graph generation, and proactive emergency push notifications. These systems possess the capability to automatically generate comprehensive intelligent emergency plans for disaster reduction [20]. Additionally, a production-oriented intelligent service system has been developed that provides warnings, decision-making support, and real-time personalized guidance for severe weather conditions [21]. The data governance framework within the context of smart cities is underpinned by theories of collaborative innovation, information lifecycle management, and digital continuity. These theoretical foundations align with the essential components of governance entities (i.e., government, enterprises, public), governance processes (including data quality and standards, storage, analysis, openness, privacy protection), and governance objects (i.e., data). The holistic construction of this framework is informed by complex systems theory.

The key to constructing an intelligent government and enhancing governance capabilities lies in the improvement of decision-making abilities. Currently, governmental decisions often revolve around singular objectives, lacking consideration for multiple levels and departments involved. To address this issue, it is imperative to fully leverage the advantages of government data sharing and cross-system collaboration by designing a big data-driven decision support system that enables intelligent early warning in problem identification, sophisticated analysis incorporating intelligent decision factors, and dynamic decision-making during problem-solving stages.

Therefore, drawing upon decision theory, this paper aims to elucidate the practical application of information science, crisis management, and decision support systems. By focusing on the fundamental issue of government crisis management and integrating multi-agent technology, our objective is to develop a multi-agent decision support system specifically tailored for government crisis management. The primary goal of this system is to enhance the efficacy of governmental crisis decision-making processes while providing comprehensive decision support for effective government crisis management.

3   Analysis of Government Crisis Decision-Making Process

The dynamic evolution of crisis events and the diversity of rescue objectives necessitate decision-makers to make timely and effective decisions that can effectively manage the escalation of crises and mitigate further losses. Furthermore, with the advent of new media platforms on the internet, crisis events often originate and disseminate from grassroots levels. However, crisis management primarily focuses on local governments, particularly county-level administrations, which have evolved into pivotal entities in decision-making processes related to crisis management. Most county-level economies exhibit a low level of development and lack robust platforms and mechanisms for expert engagement, resulting in challenges in effectively harnessing their dispersed wisdom. Consequently, government departments should analyze the crisis decision-making process and optimize it by establishing a distributed and collaborative mechanism for governmental crisis decision-making.

After a crisis event, it is of paramount theoretical and practical significance for the government to promptly and accurately discern the evolutionary patterns of the crisis, analyze the mechanisms by which decisions influence the trajectory of crisis evolution, and formulate strategies for crisis management. Scholar Zhu Xiaofeng proposed that the decision-making process in times of governmental crisis encompasses four distinct stages: perception, analysis, confirmation, and initiation. Simon categorizes this process into four stages: intelligence activities, design activities, selection activities, and implementation activities. Based on these studies, the authors contend that the decision-making process of government crisis management should integrate knowledge management and case analysis concepts to continually enhance decision-making capabilities during crisis execution.

Therefore, the decision-making process of government crisis management should be divided into two distinct stages: the stage of decision-making and the stage of decision implementation. These two stages form a closed-loop structure, wherein new knowledge must be generated following each crisis decision in order to prevent the occurrence of similar crises and mitigate any short-term actions taken by local governments that may undermine government credibility.

Therefore, the decision-making process of government crisis management should be divided into two stages: decision-making stage and decision-making implementation stage. The two stages form a closed-loop structure, that is, new knowledge should be formed after each crisis decision to prevent the occurrence of new similar crises and avoid short-term behaviors of local governments in the decision-making process to weaken government credibility. As illustrated in Fig. 1:

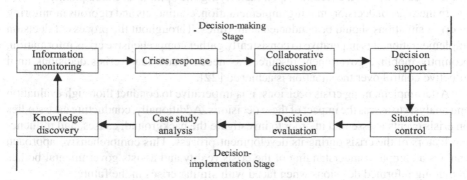

Fig. 1. Government Crisis Management Decision-making Process Diagram

3.1 Decision-Making Stage

The decision-making stage can be divided into four sequential steps: information monitoring, crisis response, collaborative discussion, and auxiliary decision-making.

The number of China's public crisis emergency response agencies, such as the State Flood Control and Drought Relief Headquarters and the National Forest Fire Prevention Headquarters, is substantial. However, the crisis data remains scattered across various departmental information systems without a dedicated department responsible for information collection, analysis, and processing. Therefore, attention needs to be given to enhance information monitoring efforts.

Information collection personnel utilize information technology to gather crisis-related multi-source heterogeneous data dispersed across various departments, subsequently processing and organizing it into a database. They employ relevant search, data mining, and other software tools for real-time monitoring of the data, ensuring timely acquisition of diverse abnormal information with utmost accuracy. After monitoring the crisis event, it swiftly transitions into the crisis response phase, during which government decision-makers must expeditiously gather accurate crisis information within a constrained timeframe.

The profound impact of public crises results in extensive damage. Bounded rationality limits the decision-making ability of an individual decision-maker. Therefore, addressing public crises necessitates collective decision-making incorporating advanced technologies such as big data, Internet of Things (IoT), and artificial intelligence (AI). Following crisis response, it is crucial to promptly transition into the stage of expert collaboration and discussion by leveraging intelligent experts and tools like machine learning for selecting optimal decision options. This approach enhances the scientific and rational nature of decision-making.

3.2 Decision Implementation Stage

Leveraging big data and artificial intelligence technology, crisis management progresses to the stage of decision execution upon identifying the optimal decision plan.

In the stage of decision-making implementation, continuous and rigorous monitoring of crisis situations should be conducted at all times. Throughout the process of decision implementation, it is imperative to consistently gather comprehensive crisis information, promptly mobilize government resources as needed, and adapt crisis decisions until effective control over the situation is achieved [22].

After implementing crisis decisions, it is imperative to conduct thorough evaluation and analysis to assess the impact of these decisions. Additionally, conducting case studies on crisis events is essential in order to investigate the background, causes, and influencing factors of the crisis during its development process. This comprehensive approach enables a complete understanding of the crisis reality and assists governmental bodies in making informed decisions when faced with similar crises in the future.

The aforementioned two stages do not exist in isolation, but rather form an interconnected closed-loop structure. Specifically, the outcomes of case analysis and knowledge discovery subsequent to decision implementation are subsequently utilized during the information monitoring stage, facilitating a progressive development of crisis decision-making capability.

Therefore, the design and development of an intelligent, interactive, and integrated government crisis decision support system is imperative to enhance the government's capacity for prompt response to emergency events, facilitate scientific decision-making processes, and enable effective decision tracking.

4   Construction of a Smart Government Crisis Management DSS Model based on Multi-Agent Technology

The Smart Government Crisis Management DSS Model must fulfill the objectives of each stage, including pre-crisis, crisis decision-making, and post-crisis stages, while ensuring the timely and accurate generation of decision-making outcomes.

Firstly, to ensure the timeliness of government crisis decision-making, it can be achieved through the collaborative work of multi-agent technology. The term "agent" typically encompasses characteristics such as autonomy, interaction, reactivity, initiative, and sociality. Agents possess the ability to accomplish intricate decision-making tasks by means of mutual coordination and negotiation. Secondly, ensuring the accuracy of government crisis decision-making necessitates pre-decision essential information monitoring and post-decision evaluation analysis. Lastly, to enhance government decision-making capabilities, it is imperative to establish a system environment conducive to knowledge discovery and mining.

The acquisition of crisis-related knowledge often stems from the handling of past crisis events. However, due to the unique nature of such events, the knowledge base in traditional decision support systems no longer suffices for meeting the demands of crisis decision-making. Consequently, it is imperative for government crisis decision support systems to establish a case base that can enhance system-wide self-learning capabilities through case analysis and knowledge discovery processes, thereby bolstering adaptability and robustness.

The author develops a distributed Multi-Agent DSS model for government crisis management, which aligns with the tasks and characteristics of each stage in the decision-making process. The Agent components within this system collaborate to achieve collaborative problem-solving, thereby enhancing the intelligence, integration, and coherence of decision making. The schematic representation of this system model is illustrated in Fig. 2.

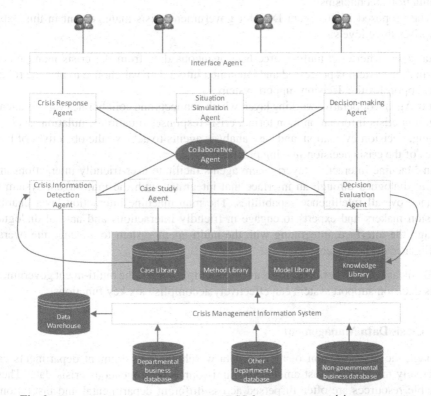

Fig. 2. Structure diagram of Multi-Agent DSS for government crisis management

In this framework, agents collaborate and employ computer intelligence technology to facilitate crisis decision-making, addressing the decision-making requirements of distributed and intricate systems while establishing a cooperative mechanism for multi-agent and multi-system interactions. The system effectively mitigates the intricacy of government crisis decision-making and faithfully replicates the entire process of such decision-making. It can effectively harness the cognitive abilities and collaborative interaction skills of multiple agents, enabling the analysis of intricate emergency crisis events, monitoring and assessment of post-decision situations, evaluation of decision outcomes, and storage of a vast array of disparate cases in the case database. The utilization of case-based reasoning technology and a case retrieval algorithm is employed to provide assistance for future crisis monitoring.

5 Model Function Analysis

Crisis decision-making falls under the category of non-procedural decision-making in an unconventional state, necessitating enhancements in both the level and quality of decision-making through improvements in crisis decision-making models and formulation mechanisms.

The proposed Multi-Agent DSS for government crisis management in this paper comprises three levels:

-Data layer: where the multi-source heterogeneous data from the crisis management information system is processed and integrated into a data warehouse to provide robust data support for the decision support system;
-Multi-Agent cooperative working layer: which connects and collaborates various agents including crisis information monitoring, crisis response, situation simulation, decision making, decision evaluation, and case analysis agents to achieve the objectives of both stages of the crisis decision-making process;
-Man-Machine interaction layer: where agents facilitate user-friendly interactions and natural dialogues through an interface that integrates with the multi-agent system to enhance overall intelligence capabilities. The man-machine interaction layer enables decision makers and experts to engage in friendly interactions and natural dialogues through the interface, integrating with the multi-agent system to enhance the overall intelligence of the system.

By means of collaborative efforts among multiple agents, the multi-agent government crisis decision support system can effectively accomplish six key functions.

5.1 Crisis Data Management

Through the establishment of a crisis data warehouse, government departments can effectively manage the vast amount of multi-source heterogeneous crisis data. These valuable resources are often dispersed across different departmental and institutional databases, hindering accessibility. The level and extent of informatization construction vary among institutions and government departments at all levels, resulting in low efficiency in retrieving and utilizing crisis data.

The construction of this decision support system is based on the data support provided by the government crisis management information system. It is imperative for all government departments to enhance their awareness of crisis management, thoroughly clean and organize key and sensitive data pertaining to crises, and import it into the crisis management data warehouse. Furthermore, the system should conduct comprehensive demand analysis, categorize various problems that may arise during the process of making crisis-related decisions according to subject matter, and establish a dedicated government crisis management data warehouse.

5.2 Crisis Information Monitoring

The Crisis Information Monitoring Agent triggers the Crisis Response Agent and collaborates with the Cooperative Agent to accomplish early crisis decision monitoring. The challenge faced by government crisis decision-making lies in effectively managing the spread of crises within limited time, information, and resources. The multi-agent distributed cooperation mode offers a solution to address collaboration issues among diverse agents through collaborative efforts.

The Crisis Information Monitoring Agent is well-suited for analyzing the changing trends of crisis data within vast repositories, enabling the study of patterns in crisis event occurrences and facilitating proactive information monitoring to prevent such events. The integration of big data, cloud computing, and artificial intelligence technologies has made it feasible to collect, process, and analyze crisis-related information.

5.3 Crisis Decision Making

The ideal state of government crisis management decision-making is to achieve coordination and cooperation among multiple entities. While crisis information is monitored by a crisis information monitoring agent prior to government crisis decision-making, certain unforeseeable and unpreventable events may still occur. In the event of a crisis, the crisis response agent can initiate an emergency plan, while the cooperative agent can mobilize experts from various regions to gather decision-making plans for sudden public crises, thereby facilitating expert intelligence. The decision-making agent collaborates with local government departments and works in conjunction with the Cooperative Agent to identify the optimal decision plan.

5.4 Crisis Situation Simulation

Prior to crisis decision-making, the Situation Simulation Agent can effectively simulate the impact of each decision plan and monitor its implementation, thereby ensuring both the manageability of decision execution and enhancing the precision of decision-making. During the implementation process, the Situation Simulation Agent can also track the evolving trends of crisis events and promptly acquire situational information. When necessary, collaborative Agents can work with experts to modify crisis decisions for better crisis control.

The Situation Simulation Agent utilizes simulation technology to generate a response plan based on environmental requirements, subsequently adjusting decisions, monitoring decision implementation, and timely adapting the decision plan to enhance the government's crisis management capabilities.

5.5 Crisis Decision Evaluation

Decision evaluation Agent can help decision-makers to better analyze decisions, analyze and measure indicators such as information consistency and result reliability of crisis decisions, reduce the uncertainty of decisions, and ensure that government decision-makers can make scientific and reasonable decisions in a dynamic, changeable and uncertain crisis environment. The decision evaluation Agent will also use various algorithms in machine learning to extract and summarize decision knowledge, store high-quality decision knowledge into the knowledge base of the crisis decision support system, and provide new knowledge and ideas for cross-region, cross-department and multi-agent collaborative knowledge mining.

The government employs digital thinking, concepts, strategies, resources, tools, and rules to govern the information space of society and deliver crisis management services of high quality in order to enhance public satisfaction. This process signifies a novel approach to governmental management and service that aims at promoting citizen-centric crisis management services while enhancing governance efficiency.

5.6 Crisis Case Analysis and Knowledge Discovery

By incorporating a case base, the case analysis Agent acquires case knowledge through the utilization of case-based reasoning technology in the field of artificial intelligence. It employs weight acquisition and an enhanced similarity algorithm based on fusion conditional probability, working in collaboration with the crisis information monitoring Agent to promptly identify crisis information. The investigation of a crisis event can commence from its background, causes, and influencing factors during its development process to conduct incident analysis and reconstruct the actuality of the crisis. This facilitates comprehensive case studies that compensate for informational deficiencies among decision-makers and aids in scientific emergency decision-making for subsequent similar events.

The case-based reasoning decision method can effectively address the challenge of crisis decision making that involves fragmented information, which is difficult to acquire knowledge about, and enhance the autonomous learning capability of crisis decision making. The evaluation and analysis conducted after implementing this decision method will facilitate continuous learning and innovation within government departments, thereby improving the scientific and rational nature of decision making. Furthermore, it will enhance the adaptability of government crisis decision support systems while reducing their vulnerability.

6 Conclusions

Effective crisis decision-making necessitates the involvement of experts from diverse government departments and disciplines, alongside the imperative utilization of advanced technology and methodologies. From a governmental perspective, a smart government transcends mere digitization and electronation of administrative processes; it primarily entails establishing an internet-based virtual government with data at its core.

A smart government leverages cutting-edge information and communication technologies, such as cloud computing, big data, and artificial intelligence, to achieve precise social governance and scientific decision-making by seamlessly integrating the virtual society with the physical world. This entails restructuring governmental organizational frameworks, reengineering administrative procedures, optimizing service provision, promoting fundamental changes in governmental concepts, approaches, methods, tools etc., and facilitating comprehensive digitization of economic and social operations to establish a novel form of governance.

The implementation of Multi-Agent DSS in government crisis management will significantly enhance the decision-making environment and capabilities of government decision support. This study commences with an analysis of the governmental crisis decision-making process, employing a collaborative framework consisting of Interface Agent, Crisis Information Monitoring Agent, Crisis Response Agent, Situation Simulation Agent, Decision Making Agent, Decision Evaluation Agent, Case Analysis Agent, and Collaboration Agent.

A theoretical model of Multi-Agent DSS for government crisis management is developed to enhance decision-making challenges arising from the distributed, real-time, and complex nature of government crisis decision making. The key innovation of this study lies in augmenting the case base within the traditional decision support system's four-library structure through collaborative efforts among multiple agents. Additionally, by incorporating case-based reasoning methods from the field of artificial intelligence, this research aims to enhance the flexibility of the government crisis decision support system.

Due to space constraints, only a conceptual model of the system is proposed in this paper. The future will witness continued exploration of models and algorithms suitable for government crisis decision support systems, alongside the conduction of simulation research on such systems.

Acknowledgements. This article acknowledges funding from the following projects:

Natural Science Foundation Project of Shandong Province (ZR2022MG074): Research on the strategy and path of realizing the value of Government Open Data based on multi-agent evolutionary game;

Shandong Key Research and Development Plan (Soft Science) Project (2021RKY01013) : Research on the advantages, challenges and strategies of Open Government Data service in Shandong Province.

References

1. Droll, Y.: Policymaking under Adversity. Chinese Academy of Governance Press, Peking (2009)
2. Xin, L.Y., Bi, Q.: Review on government crisis information management and decision-making mechanism. Libr. Inf. Work **56**(17), 15–20 (2012)
3. Zhu, X.F., Pan, Y., Zhang, R.R.: Research on government decision support system of crisis management. Inf. Sci. **25**(2), 167–172 (2007)
4. Lu, H.J., Li, Z.Q.: Empirical research on government decision-making information mechanism based on Network public opinion log mining. Libr. Constr. **10**(6), 52–56 (2014)
5. Zhang, F.Y., Lu, H.J.: Functional design of network public opinion government affairs working platform based on government decision-making information behavior. Libr. Sci. Res. **21**(5), 22–28 (2014)
6. Tan, B.Y., Wang, X.C., Lv, Y.Z.: Research on government information resource management based on government decision-making. Theory Explor. **32**(04), 37–40 (2009)
7. Liu, Y.: Knowledge management system architecture of consulting institutions oriented to government decision-making. J. Inf. **07**, 83–87 (2007)
8. Chen, J.: Construction of government public decision support information system. Inf. Inf. Work **05**, 61–66 (2012)
9. Huang, W., Xin, L.Y., Zeng, M.M.: Research on public crisis information management model for government crisis decision-making. Libr. Inf. Work **56**(17), 26–30 (2012)
10. Wen, Z.Q.: Research on Innovation of emergency decision-making mode under the perspective of government function transformation. Manage. World **5**(2), 176–177 (2016)
11. Liang, B.: Research on existing problems and countermeasures of service-oriented government decision-making mechanism in China. Theoret. Discuss. **06**(06), 35–39 (2016)
12. Chen, L.T., Zhang, C.H., Zhang, C.: Research on case-based reasoning mechanism in collaborative business environment. Fudan J. (Nat. Sci.) **44**(06), 1009–1015 (2005)
13. Liang, C.Y., Gu, D.X., Cheng, W.J., Yang, C.H., Gu, Z.Z.: Decision knowledge discovery in multi-attribute cases with discontinuous information. China Manage. Sci. **22**(04), 83–91 (2014)
14. Ma, M., Mao, J., Li, G.: From weak signal to opportunity: research progress on weak signal. Libr. Inf. Work **67**(19), 121–132 (2023)
15. Li, Y., Sun, J.J.: Construction and scenario-based application of emergency management information engineering service mechanism in complex situations. J. Inf. Inf. **41**(2), 107–117 (2022)
16. Luan, Y., Zhang, H.T., Pang, Y.F., et al.: Research on the construction of intelligent government intelligence decision system for major emergencies. Inf. Theory Pract. **46**(03), 51–59 (2023)
17. Gil, G.J.R., Dawes, S.S., Pardo, T.A.: Digital government and public management research: finding the crossroads. Publ. Manag. Rev. **20**(5), 633–646 (2018)
18. Xing, Z.J., Zhang, J.J.: Research on accurate supply of Internet + local government services – based on the survey of random photo projects in Shanxi. Chin. Adm. Adm. **09**(09), 155–157 (2019)
19. Ding, B.T.: Challenges and countermeasures of government data governance – a case study of Shanghai. Inf. Theory Pract. **42**(05), 45–49 (2019)
20. Xu, S.H., Liu, J.P., Liu, M., et al.: Research on integrated intelligent service system for disaster reduction. Sci. Surv. Mapping **44**(06), 273–278 (2019)
21. Sun, Z.G., Wang, Y.S., Zhang, L., et al.: Design and implementation of intelligent service system for monitoring and warning of facility agro-meteorological disasters in North China. Trans. Chin. Soc. Agric. Eng. **34**(23), 149–156 (2018)

Author Index

© The Editor(s) (if applicable) and The Author(s), under exclusive license
to Springer Nature Switzerland AG 2024
K. Ye and L.-J. Zhang (Eds.): ICIOT 2023, LNCS 14208, p. 101, 2024.
https://doi.org/10.1007/978-3-031-51734-1

Printed in the United States
by Baker & Taylor Publisher Services

Printed in the United States
by Baker & Taylor Publisher Services